Student comments from the Chakra Intensive Workshop upon which this book is based:

'Turning the Wheels of Life' was truly a life altering experience. I can honestly say that the quality of my life has improved since taking the course and incorporating some of the exercises into my daily routine. While my exposure to the chakras had been minimal prior to this course, I found it provided a framework for some phenomena that had just gone unexplained before. What I learned has influenced every aspect of my life including family, professional, and even personal health. An experience well worth the investment.

—Carmalita Marshall Kemayo, MA/LMFCC

The Chakra Intensive is a truly transformational journey. As I traveled through each Chakra in turn, I became aware of ways to make positive changes in my life. This is a journey I would gladly repeat and whole-heartedly recommend to all who wish to transform themselves.

—Jessica Weiss

I began to feel some changes—a little more confidence, a little more connection, maybe a little more control. I was very aware of relationships with people opening up.

—David Isler, Dispatcher

It was an all-encompassing journey in the healing and transforming of oneself.

—Cathy Eberle

The Sevenfold Journey

Reclaiming Mind, Body & Spirit
Through the Chakras

by Anodea Judith
& Selene Vega

The Crossing Press Freedom, CA 95019

Book design by Sheryl Karas
Cover design by Anne Marie Arnold
Photographs by Judith O'Connor
Cover art by Anodea Judith

Printed in the U.S.A.

2nd printing, 1995

Library of Congress Cataloging-in-Publication Data

Judith, Anodea, 1952-
        The sevenfold journey : reclaiming mind, body & spirit through
the chakras / by Anodea Judith & Selene Vega.
                        p.   cm.
        Includes bibliographical references.
        ISBN 0-89594-600-9 (hard). — ISBN 0-89594-574-6 (pbk.)
        1. Chakras.   I. Vega, Selene. II. Title.
BF1442.C53J82 1993
131—dc20   92-35719
                                                            CIP

Acknowledgements

First and foremost, we would like to acknowledge all our students from the Nine-Month Chakra Intensives, who were the trusting and enthusiastic guinea pigs for the development of this material. We thank them for the courage, honesty and willingness to be vulnerable as they wrapped their minds, bodies and spirits around the challenge of remodeling their chakras. This also extends to our clients who have shared their lives and demonstrated the effects of both childhood damage and subsequent healing as they struggled through recovery. We also want to acknowledge the support of LIFEWAYS, the organization that sponsored the Chakra Intensive year after year, allowing us to expand and time-test the material.

For the amazingly good-natured moral and technical support whenever we needed it, we thank René Vega. He kept our computers talking to each other, our backs rubbed and our graphics clear, as well as providing his beautiful male body for the photographs. Also thanks to Richard Ely for consistent kind and loving support and for taking the class the first year.

To Judith O'Connor, our photographer, we send appreciation for being patient and lovely to work with. Jaida N'ha Sandra's creative use of Anodea's first book as a workbook planted the idea for this work, and Diana Paxson's Kaballah class inspired the Chakra Intensive. B.K.S. Iyengar's knowledge and inspiration informed Selene's understanding of yoga. Also, thanks to Llewellyn Publications, for publishing *Wheels of Life*, which expanded our opportunities to teach about chakras.

And finally, to our publishers, Elaine and John Gill, who are a delight to work with, and to Julie Feingold, who connected us with Crossing Press. Thanks to you all.

To:

*Our students and clients
and their healing
journeys*

Contents

Introduction

Getting Started

For many years now we have been leading groups of people through an exciting, upward journey through the chakras. The first time we made this journey, we offered the material in a weekly class. One chakra per week, with a week of introduction and a week to wrap it up, seemed simple enough. But each night the classes would end later and later, answering questions, processing people's reactions, creating more take-home practices. We soon realized that the Chakra System itself is so profound, with the subject matter of each chakra bringing up so much personal material from each student, that we had to allow people a minimum of one month for each level in order to absorb it all. Even so, some levels, first chakra grounding for example, take much longer. Other chakras take longer for different people because they have special interests or deeper issues in that area.

From this experience the *Nine Month Chakra Intensive* evolved. For the last six years we have focused and fused, muscled and mused our way up and down the chakra ladder, creating and re-creating new and different teaching materials. This book is a compilation of those materials. With this book, you can go through the process at your own pace, spending longer on the chakras that need the attention and being the master of your own spiritual growth program. Our goal is integration—of the body and mind, spiritual and practical, inner and outer. Through healing ourselves, we heal the world around us.

What follows is a step-by-step approach to a profound spiritual system. Working in this system is not merely a matter of understanding, but of integrating that understanding into all the workings of your life. At the ground level of the first chakra we ask you to clean out your closets, start a garden or get a massage. In the second chakra we ask you to go swimming, make a change, record your emotional patterns; in the fifth chakra, to write a poem or a song. It is our feeling that spirituality can and must be part of our daily lives.

Each level brings up an immense amount of personal material and produces a transformational amount of growth. The first hour of each of our classes is set aside for the students to share with the group their work with the chakra and exercises of the previous month and the issues that came up for them. We find this process of support so valuable that we decided to include a sampling of the statements people have made so you can see the kind of issues others work through in each of the chakras. (Names used are just pseudonyms.) We encourage anyone working with this book to engage in dialogue about your own experiences as much as you can. A journal is strongly suggested, and you will find many journal exercises herein. Going on the journey with a friend or a small group will allow you to enact these discussions as you go along, giving support and feedback to each other where you need it. Sharing your experiences as you work through this book is very important even if you don't have someone traveling the path with you. The feedback and appreciation of another person will be a powerful affirmation of your work. If you are presently working with a therapist, inform him or her of your plans to work on the chakras and ask for this kind of assistance.

This is not a book to read from cover to cover and place on your shelf. Take your time. Make it a practice to savor each exercise, to isolate it long enough to feel which is the most effective for you. It is so common for people in our culture to rush through, grasp at the beginnings of understanding, but never delve deeply.

We want you to enjoy the process of working on yourself. There is no contest here, no grades, no examination or standard of achievement. There is no point at which you are "there," having mastered it all. In the fifteen years Anodea has been working with the chakras, and the eight that Selene has joined her, we are still learning or opening something new every time we teach this course.

It takes a little more initiative to travel this path without a class. In class we provide music and materials and lead the exercises, meditations and ceremonies. In this book we include discography, pictures of the exercises, and instructions for setting up the rituals, but you must do them on your own. However, the class we have taught only meets one time per month, and the bulk of the responsibility has always been with the students. Keep in mind that the exercises are cumulative. Practicing them once is merely an introduction. Practicing them daily for a period of time can effect profound changes in the way your body feels and the way you interact with others. Awareness of the issues connected with these exercises helps to bring body and mind together in an enlightening experience.

In this book you will find a variety of techniques, ranging from meditations and journal exercises to rituals and political activism. Some of them you will find more effective or appealing than others, depending on who you are and what your general preferences are. You may be the type of person who prefers to work alone, or who prefers to work with others. Some of the exercises are designed for partners or groups, and if you are not working with a group or partner formally, you may want to think of a few friends to try these with. Some people gravitate toward the physical and shun the mental, while others are quite the opposite. Generally speaking, we encourage you to do what works best for you. There is a tendency, however, for each of us to gravitate toward what comes easiest and avoid the areas where we need the most work. Being a mentally-oriented, peaceful type, you might love the meditation and hate the physical exercises. Be aware that the physical exercises may be what brings you the most benefit, once you get over the initial resistance. Working with the Chakra System supplies us with a multi-dimensional system that requires development and integration of physical, emotional, mental and spiritual states. Our goal is to bring these different levels into balance.

Some of the techniques we will use include journal exercises, meditations, physical exercises, rituals, interactive exercises, discussions, mundane assignments, and art, music, dance or writing projects. Which of these holds the most immediate appeal for you? Notice which ones seem less attractive, or even repugnant. Take some time to reflect on just what it is you dislike. Is meditation too boring? If so, what is your need for excitement? Do the physical exercises seem intimidating? If so, to whose standards are you holding yourself? Do the tasks seem overwhelming? If so, how did you get your life so busy that it doesn't allow time for your spiritual practices? Answering these questions for yourself is an integral part of this work.

Understanding the Concept

Each chakra is symbolized by a multi-petaled lotus, the number of petals varying with the chakra. These lotuses are taken from diagrams of ancient texts.

The Chakra System is an ancient metaphysical system that diagrams the interrelationship between various aspects of our multidimensional universe. As part of this universe, we too are multidimensional. We have bodies, emotions, thoughts, ideas, actions. We live in a world with communities and governments, technology and history, and we ponder the mysteries of earth and sky, spirit and matter, here and hereafter. We are as complex as the world around us.

The Chakra System addresses that complexity in a simple and systematic way. We can "work on ourselves" in a step-by-step fashion—a way that is practical and direct, yet profound. To do this we will work on one chakra at a time, yet each chakra is always influenced by the others.

This section will give you an overview of the Chakra System as a whole, so that you have an idea of the basic territory before you begin on the journey. Because we are presenting an experiential approach in this book, this overview is brief. If you would like more in-depth information, we refer you to Anodea's previous "chakra textbook," *Wheels of Life: A User's Guide to the Chakra System*, published by Llewellyn Publications, 1987.

What is a chakra?

Originating from within the ancient yoga systems of India, chakras refer to spinning vortices of energy created within us by the interpenetration of consciousness and the physical body. Through this combination, chakras become *centers of activity for the reception, assimilation and transmission of life energies*. Technically, the word is from the Sanskrit language and translates as *wheel* or *disk*. We can think of them as spheres of energy radiating from the central nerve ganglia of the spinal column.

Correspondences

There are seven major chakras within each of us, arranged vertically from the base of the spine to the top of the head, centered, more or less, through the middle of our body. In addition to the nerve ganglia, they also correspond to glands in the endocrine system, and various bodily processes, such as breathing, digesting or procreating. Archetypally they represent the elemental forces of earth, water, fire, air, sound, light and thought. These elements are a metaphorical representation of the energetic expression of each chakra—earth that is solid, heavy, and dense; water that flows; fire that radiates and transforms; air that is soft; sound that communicates; light that reveals; thoughts that store information.

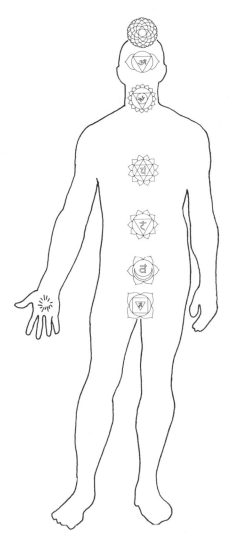

Numerous other correspondences have been attributed to the chakras, such as colors, sounds, deities, gemstones, herbs or planetary influences. Examining each of these brings us closer to the understanding of the essential nature of a particular chakra. Using gemstones, colors or herbs helps strengthen the association with the state we are seeking. A red candle, for example, may help us to remember that we want to focus on our grounding because red is the color associated with the first chakra and grounding is one of its goals. In this way, chakra correspondences can be used as mnemonic devices. We include a general table of correspondences here and a smaller one at the beginning of each subsequent chapter. (See next page.)

Psychologically, the chakras correspond to major areas of our lives (from bottom to top): survival, sex, power, love, communication, imagination and spirituality. If we take the literal meaning of the word chakra (disk) and give it a modern interpretation, we can think of a chakra as a psychic "floppy disk" that contains programming about how to handle various aspects of our life. These floppy disks plug into the "hardware" of our physical bodies, and are interpreted by the "operating system" of our basic consciousness.

The base chakra, for example, contains our "survival" program, such as what diet suits us best, when we need to exercise or sleep, and how to take care of ourselves when we're sick. The second chakra contains our programming about sexuality and emotions—how we handle emotional states, our sexual orientation and preferences. The fourth chakra contains our programming about relationships. We each have a slightly different model of hardware, programmed in a distinct language with unique operating systems. We work with the chakras to get the bugs out of the programs, and get the whole system up and running smoothly.

Table of Correspondences

	Chakra One	Chakra Two
Sanskrit Name	Muladhara	Svadhisthana
Meaning	Root	Sweetness
Location	Base of spine, coccygeal plexus, legs, feet, large intestine	Abdomen, genitals, low back, hips
Element	Earth	Water
Main Issue	Survival	Sexuality, emotions
Goals	Stability, grounding, prosperity, right livelihood, physical health	Fluidity, pleasure, relaxation
Malfunction	Obesity, hemmorhoids, constipation, sciatica, anorexia, knee troubles, bone disorders, frequent illness in general, frequent fears, inability to focus, "spaciness," inability to be still	Stiffness, sexual problems, isolation, emotional instability or numbness
Color	Red	Orange
Celestial Body	Saturn	Moon
Foods	Proteins, meats	Liquids
Right	To have	To feel
Stones	Garnet, hematite, bloodstone, lodestone	Coral, carnelian
Animals	Elephant, ox, bull	Fish, alligator
Operating Principle	Gravity	Attraction of opposites
Yoga Path	Hatha Yoga	Tantra Yoga
Archetypes	Earth Mother	Eros

Table of Correspondences

Chakra Three	Chakra Four	Chakra Five
Manipura	Anahata	Vissudha
Lustrous gem	Unstruck	Purification
Solar plexus	Heart	Throat
Fire	Air	Sound
Power, energy	Love	Communication
Vitality, strength of will, purpose	Balance, compassion, acceptance	Clear communication, creativity, resonance
Ulcers, timidity, domination, fatigue, digestive troubles	Loneliness, codependence	Sore throats, stiff neck, poor communication
Yellow	Green	Bright blue
Mars, Sun	Venus	Mercury
Carbohydrates	Vegetables	Fruit
To act	To love	To speak
Topaz, amber	Emerald, rose quartz	Turquoise
Ram, lion	Antelope, dove	Elephant, bull
Combustion	Equilibrium	Sympathetic vibration
Karma Yoga	Bhakti Yoga	Mantra Yoga
Magician	Quan Yin	Hermes

Table of Correspondences

	Chakra Six	_Chakra Seven_
Sanskrit Name	Ajna	Sahasrara
Meaning	To perceive	Thousandfold
Location	Brow	Top of head
Element	Light	Thought
Main Issue	Intuition	Understanding
Goals	Psychic perception, imagination	Wisdom, knowledge, spiritual connection
Malfunction	Headaches, nightmares, hallucinations	Confusion, apathy, overly intellectual
Color	Indigo Blue	Violet
Celestial Body	Neptune	Uranus
Foods	Feasts for the eyes!	None, fasting
Right	To see	To know
Stones	Lapis lazuli	Amethyst
Animals	Owl, butterfly	Elephant, ox, bull
Operating Principle	Projection	Consciousness
Yoga Path	Yantra Yoga	Jnana Yoga
Archetypes	Hermit, Psychic, Dreamer	Sage, Wisewoman

Additional Chakras

In addition to the seven major chakras that we focus on here, there are smaller chakras in the hands and feet, knees, fingertips, shoulders, etc. These are also meeting points of energy pathways traveling through the body, but they do not have major philosophical associations. They are, instead, extensions of the major chakras. The hands are connected to third, fourth, and fifth chakras, and the feet to chakra one. Yet, someone who works with their hands will want to develop their hand chakras, and good, solid grounding must include opening the chakras in the feet.

Hand Chakra Opening

The easiest way to experience what a chakra feels like is through opening the hand chakras.

1 Extend both arms out in front of you, parallel to the floor with elbows straight. Turn one hand up and one hand down.

2 Now quickly open and close your hands twenty times or so. Turn your palms the opposite way and repeat. This opens the hand chakras.

3 To feel them, open your hands and slowly bring your palms together, starting about two feet apart and moving slowly to a distance of a few inches. When your hands are about four inches apart you should be able to feel a subtle ball of energy, like a magnetic field, floating be-tween your palms. If you tune in closely, you may even be able to feel the chakras spinning. After a few moments the sensation will decrease, but you can create it again by repeating the steps above.

The energy you feel between your hands in this exercise also runs through your arms, legs, torso and organs at all times. With practice, you can learn to feel the other chakras.

Energy Currents

Because humans are upright creatures, taller than we are wide, our major energy currents flow up and down the body. We can think of ourselves as a tube that receives and discharges energy from either end. Therefore, that which is received from the top of the tube will flow downward to the base, and that which enters from the bottom will flow upward towards the crown.

So too with the Chakra System. Thoughtforms entering consciousness work their way down through the chakras until they hit the base chakra (element earth, or the manifested form of the earth plane). At each level the thoughtform becomes more specific and more dense. An idea becomes a picture in the mind, then words spoken, an action expressed, a result produced. This downward current is called the *Path of Manifestation*. Through the condensation of ethereal forms, we take something abstract and bring it into the concrete.

Alternately, the path that moves upward from the base chakra is called the *Path of Liberation*. Along this pathway, that which is bound to a form is gradually freed from the form to encompass greater scope and abstraction. Thus we burn wood to produce fire and heat, and the light of the fire lives on in our minds. Energy stored within matter is released.

It is our firm opinion that both of these currents need to be equally developed for a person to be fully functional in today's world. Poor grounding as a result of blockage in the downward current can result in poor concentration, health problems, economic troubles, and being out of touch with our effects on others. A poorly developed Path of Liberation can result in the feeling of being stuck in a rut, boredom, tyranny, depression, inability to get off the ground, and lack of vitality.

There are a third and fourth current, created from the combination of the first two. These are the currents of *Reception* and *Expression* that occur through the chakras themselves as they interact with the outside world. You can think of the tube as having little holes in it like a flute. The holes that are covered or open dictate the overall sound that the flute makes. Likewise the open and closed chakras create the overall sense of self that we present to the rest of the world. What is blocked off can neither receive nor express. In order to make different sounds, we want to consciously control the opening and closing of each chakra.

Understanding Blockages

Chakras can be energetically *excessive* or *deficient*, terms used in Chinese acupuncture to describe the behavior of organ meridians. A deficient chakra can be thought of as a chakra that is closed—it has very little energy traveling through it. Physiologically, a chakra is like a bundle of nerve fibers. When there is little energy traveling through the bundle, it tends to collapse. Think of how your heart feels when you are depressed—it's as if your chest collapses. The body shapes itself around the fullness or emptiness of a chakra, and we can often deduce the state of a chakra from simply examining the body structure.

When a chakra is deficient, you might say that the programming is locked in a *restrictive* pattern, habitually blocking out incoming stimulation. It cannot take in. This means that the kind of activity associated with that chakra (i.e. sexuality, power, communication) is also blocked in one's life. There are usually physical signs that give additional indication of blocked chakras—such as impotence, ulcers, or stiff neck (related to chakras 2, 3, and 5 respectively).

An excessive chakra is also blocked but for a different reason. Think of it as the table top in your home that collects everything. It's too cluttered to be fully functional. Energetically speaking, an excessive chakra does not know how to let go. Again the programming is fixed in a restrictive pattern, but this one restricts internal energy from being expressed, whereas the deficient chakra restricts external energy from coming in. When internal energy is not released, the issue related to that chakra becomes a constant dominating force in the system as a whole. So, an excessive third chakra creates a bully, or one who always has to be in control, often at the cost of love, pleasure or understanding; an excessive second chakra manifests as sexual addiction, or the filtering of all exchanges through a sexual framework. An excessive first chakra might lead to the hoarding of possessions, food, or money. Excess and deficiency also run through the system as a whole, seeking an overall balance which may need readjustment. An excessive fifth chakra (such as talking too much) might be balancing a deficient second chakra (sexual frustration).

It is possible for a chakra to be excessive in some aspects and deficient in others—in other words, out of balance within itself. One might hoard possessions but be anorexic. Both states are a reaction to past programming, coping mechanisms, or trauma around the issues of survival.

If a chakra is deficient or excessive, it creates a blockage in the central stream of energy through the body. The downward current cannot make it all the way to manifestation, nor can the upward current make it all the way to liberation. Where the chakra blockages occur explains a lot about us as people. If our chakras are blocked in the second or third levels, for example, the Path of Liberation is restricted. We would tend to be grounded to a degree but resistant to change and growth. If there is blockage in chakras five or six, the Liberating current gets going well, but the Manifesting current doesn't go very far. We might be full of ideas but vague and scattered, and seldom able to bring our ideas to fruition.

These energy patterns give us the classic characters of people who are primarily "in their heads" or who are very physical or anti-intellectual. A block in the heart chakra might appear more balanced, but there is a severance between mind and body. Blocks in the base or crown chakras create the strongest imbalances—the energy doubles back on itself without completing its transformation. (See diagrams.)

The blockage in one chakra may be affected by overall patterns in the upward and downward currents. An activity related to that chakra would be either difficult to manifest at all, or would manifest with frequent problems, especially ones that repeat themselves. For example, a heart chakra blockage might result in

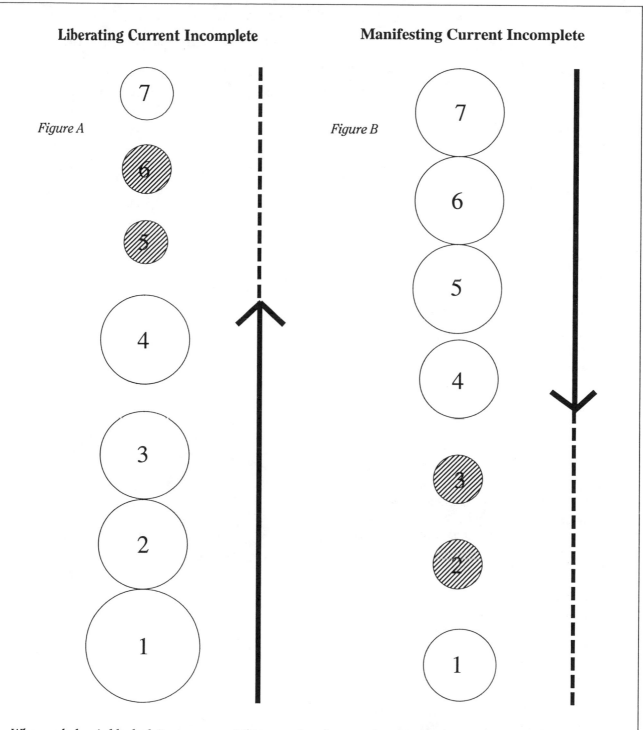

Liberating Current Incomplete

Manifesting Current Incomplete

Figure A

Figure B

When a chakra is blocked, it may prevent the upward or downward current from completing its journey, thereby leaving a chakra behind the blockage (such as chakra seven in figure A, or chakra one in figure B) undernourished. This results in a chakra that is deficient, but may not otherwise be blocked.

Manifesting Current Incomplete

Chakra blockage can also occur through a chakra that is excessive. Too much of the overall energy is taken up by a particular chakra, in this case, chakra three. The manifesting energy which is trying to come down from the top gets absorbed by the excessive chakra to the detriment of the ones below, which are left deficient. This can happen with both manifesting and liberating currents. Excessive chakras can occur as a result of overstimulation, or as a compensation for other blocked areas.

The liberating current in this instance is almost non-existent, as there is insufficient energy to get it started. This type of person would have a fear of grounding, of being in touch with their lower body. Because of the lack of liberating energy, there is a tendency to get stuck, hence the excessive third chakra.

difficulty making relationships at all (blocked manifestation), or a tendency to repeatedly get involved in abusive relationships (blocked liberation).

What blocks a chakra?

Generally speaking, programming from childhood experiences and cultural values causes our chakras to be blocked. A child who gets beaten by his parents learns to shut out his body sensations. A child who is emotionally neglected shuts down the emotional second chakra. A culture that denies sexuality and promotes obedience to authority forces us to shut down our second and third chakras accordingly. Noise pollution, unattractive surroundings, or lies make us shut down our fifth, sixth, and seventh chakras respectively. The pain of unrequited love teaches us to close our heart. Basically, past pain or stress, whatever its source, affects the healthy functioning of our chakras. This is a simplification of a complex process, which we will explore through journal exercises herein, and more deeply in *The Psychology of the Chakras*, a work in progress.

The Seven Basic Rights

We can describe the chakras as representing seven basic rights— rights that should be ours from birth. Unfortunately, these rights are infringed upon by circumstances throughout our lives. When we learn to accept this infringement, the chakra may overcompensate (become excessive) or close down (become deficient).

Chakra One: The right to have

The underlying right of the first chakra is the right to be here. This manifests in the right to have what we need in order to survive. When we are denied the basic necessities of survival— food, clothing, shelter, warmth, medical care, healthy environment, physical touch—our rights to have are threatened. Consequently, we will be likely to question that right throughout our lives, in relation to many things, from money and possessions to love or time to ourselves.

Chakra Two: The right to feel

"Stop your crying, you have nothing to be upset about!" "You have no right to be angry." "How can you express your emotions like that? You should be ashamed of yourself!" These kinds of injunctions infringe upon our right to feel. A culture that frowns upon emotional expression, or calls someone weak for having sensitivity, also infringes on this basic right. A subcorollary of this right is the right to want. If we can't even feel, it is very difficult to know what we want.

Chakra Three: The right to act

This right is restricted by abusive authority in parents and culture. Draft resistors are arrested. Peaceful demonstrators practicing non-violence are also arrested and often abused for taking action according to their feelings about their rights to survive. We are taught to obey and to follow—that actions taken had better be correct. Fear of punishment and enforcement of blind obedience, whether from parents or culture, seriously impair our personal power—the conscious use of our right to act.

Chakra Four: The right to love and be loved

In a family, this right can be abridged when parents do not consistently and unconditionally love and care for their child. When conditions are put on love, a child's self-love is threatened. In cultural conditioning, heart chakra restriction can be seen in judgmental attitudes about men loving men and women loving women, or one race loving another, or people loving more than one person. The right to love is damaged in racial strife, dominance of one culture over another, by war, or anything that creates enmity between groups. When we get hurt or rejected we often question or restrict our right to love, and subsequently close down our hearts.

Chakra Five: The right to speak and hear truth

Difficulty here occurs when we are not allowed to speak in our family. "Don't talk to me like that, young man!" This includes not being heard when we do speak, and/or not being spoken to honestly. When we are denied expression, told to keep secrets, or maintain family lies, our fifth chakra shuts down. When we are criticized for our attempts to speak, or have our trust violated around communicating private material, we gradually lose contact with our right to speak.

Chakra Six: The right to see

This right is damaged when we are told that what we perceive is not real, when things are deliberately hidden or denied (such as father's drinking) or from having the breadth of our vision misunderstood and discounted. When what we see is ugly, frightening, or inconsistent with something else we see, our physical vision may be affected by the closing down of the third eye. Reclaiming the right to see helps us reclaim our psychic abilities as well.

Chakra Seven: The right to know

This includes the right to information, the right to truth, and the right to education and knowledge. Equally important are our spiritual rights, to connect with the Divine in whatever way we as individuals perceive it. To force on another a spiritual dogma, such as Christians dominating the Witches of Europe or tribal cultures remaining in other parts of the world, is an infringement on our seventh chakra personal rights.

The Chakras Developmentally

Development of the skills and concepts related to each chakra occurs progressively throughout life. While each chakra receives and organizes information at all times, there are developmental stages in which we focus attention primarily upon learning certain tasks. These stages are not exact and will overlap and vary from one individual to another. It is useful, however, in assessing your own chakras, to consider how these stages were supported in your life, what difficulties or traumas may have occurred, and how they may have affected the chakras that were developing at that time.

Chakra One: Second trimester to nine months

The first chakra relates to prenatal development and earliest childhood when most of a child's awareness is focused on survival and physical comfort. This is the stage of life where body growth is most rapid. The most important aspect of this development is that the child learns to feel safe, have trust in the world, and have her survival needs provided adequately.

Chakra Two: Six to twenty-four months

The next stage has its beginnings at birth but comes into the forefront between ages one and two. This is the stage of experiencing "other," of sensation, and of emotions. It is also the time when the child begins to locomote and explore the world through his senses. Beyond survival, the child needs to feel loved, experience pleasure at being alive, and have a pleasant and stimulating array of sensations to explore, such as colors and sounds, textures and tastes, and nurturing, non-invasive touch from parents and caretakers.

Chakra Three: Eighteen months to three years

Chakra Three comes into play with the period of attempted autonomy and development of will. The child is naturally self-centered, and wishes to establish a sense of personhood, power, and the ability to self-create. Mothers often call this the "terrible twos," or the "no" stage. The important issue here is to allow the child a sense of her own autonomy and an experience of her own power, as well as a healthy sense of limits based on respect rather than "power-over" on the part of the parent.

Chakra Four: Three to six years

Chakra Four develops as the child begins to find his relationship in the family and in the larger world. He begins to mimic and respond to family dynamics, and develop his own interpersonal style. Friendships and play with others become more important and peers begin to exert a subtle influence on the shaping of the personality.

Parents need to provide loving support within the family to enable the child to gradually expand his web of relationships in order to feel loved and connected with a larger world. Dysfunctional family dynamics have a particularly large impact at this age. Children need to have healthy role models for the expression of affection and love.

Chakra Five: Six to ten years

The social identity that develops in the previous years expands at this time through creative expression. The child begins, through communication, to test her understanding of the world. It is important to support creativity without judgments, and to listen attentively and communicate honestly.

Chakra Six: Seven to twelve years

Learning through communication and exploration, the child begins to form his internal picture of the world and his place within it. He moves into Chakra Six, the realm of imagination, and begins to recognize patterns, develop psychic sensitivities, and perceive what he encounters with an open mind. It is important at this stage that parents provide information and experiences without invalidating the child's perceptions. Games that employ creative imagination (for example, asking a child to project images into new scenarios through questions such as "What if?") help to develop this ability.

Chakra Seven: Twelve and up

In Chakra Seven we engage in the pursuit of knowledge—the learning, training, thinking and gathering of information. We then have a complete set of tools to process all previous and future experience. This may also be a period of spiritual exploration, although this varies from person to person. The best support for this process is a stimulating intellectual environment in the home, encouragement to question belief systems, teaching the child to think for herself, and provision of a good educational environment.

Damage that occurs during any of these crucial stages can affect the chakra that is developing at that time. As you explore the issues and imbalances in your own chakra system, added insight will come from reflecting upon your experiences during these formative stages. As a parent it is important to be aware of your difficulties with specific chakras, in order to avoid passing on your own unresolved conflicts to your children.

This workbook is about how to free your body, your life, and your basic rights through working with the Chakra System. Chakras can be developed like muscles, healed through understanding, and reprogrammed according to your wishes and needs. It is a complex system, and development of each chakra takes time and patience. Judgment of yourself or your progress is fruitless. The goal is understanding.

Establishing a Practice

This workbook will provide you with many exercises and practices to experiment with, and this is easiest if you put aside a particular time to practice. Setting up a routine schedule for working with these materials will help you in several ways. First of all, although you may start out excited and committed to practicing, there are always those days when you just want to sleep another half hour instead. It's so easy to give in to that with the promise that you'll get to the practice later at some unspecified time. Yet, in our busy lives it is difficult to find a way to haphazardly squeeze in a spiritual practice, even though we know that the benefits are worth it. Establishing a schedule enables a habit to develop, thereby eliminating the need to create the time anew each day.

Choose a time when you can work without interruption from family or phone calls and when you can put yourself into the practice fully. If you know that in the morning you feel harried and tend to focus on what you will be doing that day, then maybe the evenings or right before bed would work best for you. If you are so tired by the end of the day that you'll be half asleep if you practice before bed, then choose another time. At first, you might even try several possibilities over the course of a week or so, evaluating which works best for you.

How often you work is up to you. Consistency is the most important, but greater frequency will bring results faster. Given the same quantity of time to spend on practice, we recommend that you work more frequently for less time each session, rather than save up the time for a marathon practice once a week. Something between twenty minutes and an hour per day is a good amount of time to spend, and you may want to break this up in parts. For example, twenty minutes of movement work in the morning and twenty minutes of other activities in the evening. If, however, you can only do ten minutes, it is better to do that than none at all.

Something else to consider is where you want to practice. You will need a floor space large enough to lie down and swing your arms and legs out and around you without hitting the furniture. This may mean moving a few things over when you practice. If you live in a cramped space, choose exercises that fit into your space and then find a way to use the outdoors whenever you can. When the space we are moving in is constricted, our movements tend to be constricted as well, and you will need a way to counteract this influence for at least part of the time you establish.

We highly recommend setting up an altar that can change with your current focus. All this requires is an empty dresser top or shelf or some creative set-up that allows you to place pictures and items relating to the chakra you are working on at the time. The ideal situation is to create your altar in the same room or space that you will be practicing the physical exercises, but if this is not possible, set up your altar where you will be able to do your meditations and journal-writing, perhaps where you can see it from your bed as you awaken in the morning. We will include suggestions for each chakra's altar, but feel free to let your imagination go, so that you have a living, changing expression of the energies you are working with.

You might also consider what you will wear to practice. We usually ask our students to come to class wearing comfortable clothing that allows them to move, and, if they can, to wear the color of the chakra we are working on. The primary consideration here is that your clothing (if you choose to wear any) not restrict you in any way from moving or breathing deeply.

Working with Movement

In order to travel from one end of the chakra spectrum to the other and back again, we must be willing and able to move our energy through different configurations. As mind and body are intricately interconnected, and the chakras are points where the two connect, movement becomes an invaluable technique for successfully changing our energy patterns and our basic experience.

Movement has been used in many settings, both ancient and modern, to enhance self-awareness, group bonding, and connection with the sacred. Without our conscious attention, the ways we move and hold ourselves in day-to-day life express feelings and attitudes about ourselves, our relationship to others and to the world around us. When we pay attention to this process, we can access many things that have been hidden from the conscious mind. In addition to this wealth of information, we have the capability of two-way communication—by working with our movements, we can affect areas of ourselves that have been blocked or stagnant and begin the process of healing and reprogramming. We will be guiding you through many exercises and experiments to bring awareness, to awaken, and to create change through your body and movement.

Part of the movement work presented in this book is technical in nature, in that we provide you with specific instructions for the correct way to practice a physical movement. There are many places where we will go beyond the physical instructions into providing a framework for more spontaneous movement, but where there are specifics, they are important. For people who have been somewhat sedentary, or unused to stretching, it is important to pay attention to your limits and move up to them slowly and carefully. Practicing the poses for each chakra will do more than work on the energy of that chakra—many general principles for movement and posture in daily life are included, and you will find your body knowing more and more about how to move in a healthy fashion.

In this chapter we present some basic preliminary practices that will provide you with an introduction to your own body. Even if you are a very physical person, these exercises can bring you a greater awareness of what is happening in your body.

Every movement session should begin with some form of warm up for your body. The Body Awakening exercise can perform this function, or you may find exercises in different chakras that will work better for you. You might simply put on some music and allow yourself to spontaneously move to it but, whatever you do, use this time to pay attention to what's going on in your body at the moment. Are there stiff areas that need special attention? Is there an injured place that requires some care and awareness as you move? You will get to know your own body and its needs after working with it consistently, and can develop your own style of easing into the movement work that takes into consideration what you individually need to loosen up and prevent injury. Your personal warm up can become part of the ritual of chakra movement work—or even other chakra work that does not involve movement. Often, meditation or journal work can be smoother and easier once you have paid some attention to your body.

Deep Relaxation in Corpse Pose (Savasana)

Begin by lying down on the floor with your legs comfortably apart (about a foot and a half apart) and your arms resting about a foot away from your sides with palms face up. If you have a hard floor, lie on an exercise mat or pad or fold a blanket to create a more comfortable surface. Close your eyes, then take a deep breath and let it out, allowing your muscles to relax as the floor holds you up. Tune in to how your body is feeling on the floor. Which parts of you are heavy, sinking into the floor? Which parts of you are just lightly resting on the floor? Where are there spaces between you and the floor? Notice how your clothing feels on your body, the textures, the places that are tight or constricting, the places that feel cozy, the parts where there is no clothing and your skin is touched by the air that moves almost imperceptibly around you.

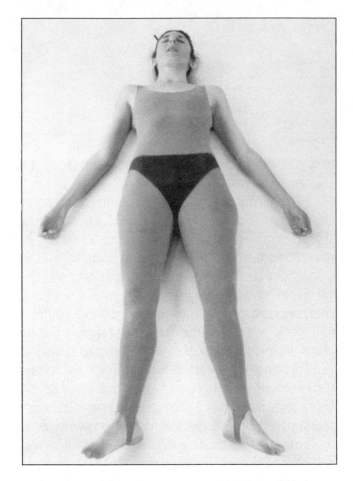

Now bring your awareness down to your feet, feeling into the muscles and joints of your feet, noticing any tension or discomfort there and allowing it to drain out of your feet into the earth, emptying your feet and leaving them quiet. Move your attention up through your ankles, into your lower legs, your calves and shins and allow any tensions there to release and drain out of your legs down into the earth. Move your awareness up through your knees and into your thighs, feeling those muscles—some of the strongest in our bodies—and letting any discomfort release and drain out of your legs down into the earth, emptying your legs and leaving them quiet and comfortable. Move your awareness up into your hip joints and around and through your genitals and buttocks and belly and feel any discomfort release and drain out of you down through your buttocks, emptying out into the earth beneath you, leaving your pelvis quiet and comfortable. Move your awareness up along the muscles of your back, on either side of your spine, allowing any tension to release and drain out of you down into the earth. Move your awareness around your waist and up into your ribs, feeling the gentle movement of your breathing, allowing any discomfort to dissolve and drain out of you down into the earth. As you release the tension in your torso, move your awareness up into your shoulders, releasing and emptying any discomfort into the earth, leaving your upper torso quiet and comfortable. Move your awareness down your arms, through your elbows and wrists and into your hands and fingers, gently releasing any tension, emptying it

Deep Relaxation (continued)

down into the earth. Move your awareness up into your neck now, feeling the strong muscles that hold up your head all day, allowing those muscles to release and drain all the tension out and down into the earth. Move your awareness into your jaw and mouth, releasing the muscles, allowing your tongue to soften, your lips to soften, your cheeks to smooth out. Feel your eyes, soft and heavy, your forehead smoothing out, your scalp loosening, releasing any tension and emptying it down into the earth through the back of your head.

Check again through your body to see if there is any tension that still needs to release and let that too drain down into the earth, leaving your entire body quiet and still, lying on the ground, relaxed.

Listen to the sounds around you, and then let those sounds become background as you move your awareness to the sounds of your own body—your breathing, digestive sounds, and perhaps even the rhythmic beat of your heart.

From here you can move into whatever work you would like to do in this relaxed state of consciousness, or you can rest here until you are ready to return to an alert state. To return, begin to breathe more deeply, allowing each breath to move through your entire body, inspiring you to stretch and yawn, reach and wiggle, until you are ready to roll onto your side and come up, ready to move into your next activity, alert and yet relaxed.

Body Awakening

When you are relaxed and your body is quiet, imagine that you have been in this state for a very long time, so long that you've lost track of how long it has been, so long that you've almost forgotten how this body of yours moves. Let your body begin to awaken, starting at your fingers, feeling energy begin to move in your fingers so that the muscles begin to work again. At first it may seem like an uncontrolled spasm, or a very slight wiggle. Take your time, playing with that movement, exploring the range of motion and strength, curling and stretching. As you move your fingers, notice that the muscles in your palms are involved in the movement. Let them explore as well, feeling the energy of movement travel up from your hands into your arms. Take your time exploring, playing, allowing the movement to travel up your arms into your shoulders, neck, head, then down into your upper torso, waist, hips and pelvis, legs, feet. Spend as much time on each awakening area as you feel like, and when your entire body has awakened, let the energy travel around, moving fast or slow, with sharp or gentle movements, rhythmic or flowing. Find a way to move your body on the floor, rocking or rolling onto your side, exploring the positions your body is capable of. Eventually you may find a way up onto your feet, dancing all the while, continuing to explore all of the movement possibilities of your body.

Find a way to end, slowing yourself down and allowing your body to come to rest in whatever position feels right. Take some time in this position to pay attention to how your body feels now, how you are breathing.

Entering Sacred Space

We see reclaiming spirituality as essential to creating a healthy balanced life. Meditation and ritual are the tools we use to reawaken this much neglected aspect of our beings.

The essence of meditation is tuning in, focusing on the absolute present moment, watching as it moves into the next moment and flows onward. There are many techniques of meditation, with roots in many traditions of spiritual practice, but generally the observation of the moment-to-moment flow of the present is a key feature. Sometimes this defines the entire meditation, with no other goal, no other focus. Other times, there is a focus, a theme or idea that we are attempting to position at the center of that moment-to-moment flow. The meditations in this workbook often follow this format, creating a mind-space within which to work on a particular thought, feeling, concept, or visualization. Our minds may wander from this theme we are working with, but we can bring them back and focus them in the present moment on the image at hand (without judgment or guilt about the loss of focus).

Our concept of ritual starts from the same process that shapes meditation—an awareness of flow. Meditation becomes ritual by virtue of the small habitual patterns we develop to frame our meditation practice. This could be as simple as closing the door of your room and lighting a stick of incense. It could be even simpler, involving merely placing your body in a particular position and beginning to focus in. It could also be quite elaborate, requiring various musical instruments, appropriate garb, candles, a particular sacred space that you reserve only for doing this work, or various other people to participate in some way.

Ritual acts provide a signal to the body to begin the physiological and energetic changes that are part of the practice. Often, breathing changes as we perform the familiar ritual. These small changes are part of opening to larger changes in our lives. We use the powerful techniques of ritual to help initiate these changes, aiming for an altered state of consciousness conducive to self-exploration and reprogramming.

There are many ways to practice ritual, and many differences in the rituals around the world. For each chakra we have provided some ideas to get you started. Don't limit yourself to our ideas; use your creativity. Take the tasks, movement practices, journal writing, music listening, book reading, and whatever else comes to mind, to create your own rituals of whatever length works for you. All the exercises, physical or otherwise, are pieces you can use in ritual if you find them useful. Pay attention to how each affects you and use those which alter your consciousness that way when you want that effect.

There are some basics that may help you in organizing your practices and ideas into rituals. The most important one to remember involves the creation of a sacred space within which to work. Use the suggestions for establishing a practice to help you choose and set up a place for your rituals. Then create the space in time through the use of a specific beginning and ending to delineate the boundaries of your ritual. This can be done through words that you say, gestures performed, a specific posture taken, or simply closing your eyes and tuning in to how you are feeling at that moment. Some traditions use the calling of the directions to establish sacred space, while others physically draw or visualize a circle or sphere around the participants and the place they are working. Others have a specific prayer, song or chant that they use to begin or end. At the end of the ritual, it's important to undo what you've done to create sacred space. If you've invited elements or deities to join you, make sure to acknowledge them and let them know that you are done and are releasing them from the container of sacred space that you created for this ritual.

Mindfulness

To give you an experience of meditation in its simplest form, here is an exercise that you can perform anywhere, in almost any situation.

Close your eyes and hold the position your body is in. Bring your attention to your body, the pose you are sitting, standing or lying in. Notice the parts of you that are touching the floor, which muscles are working to keep you in this position, where the strains and discomforts are. If you need to release tension, or rearrange your position now that you are aware of any discomforts, go ahead and do so. Continue to pay attention to bodily sensations as you open your eyes and continue with whatever you need to do next. Follow each movement with awareness, follow each thought with awareness. Keep your thoughts focused on the present, and when they wander, notice them wandering and bring them back, letting go of the impulse to judge yourself or get impatient with yourself. Just gently bring your attention back to the moment, back to the flow of the present.

Journal Exercises

One of the best ways to chart your journey on the path of self-exploration and healing is to keep a journal. Putting your experiences, thoughts and emotions on paper enables you to sort through the contents of your mind and begin to see the patterns that flow through your life.

Many of the exercises in this book will generate thoughts and feelings and provide a jumping off point for writing. In addition, we will provide specific ideas for journal writing for each of the chakras. Once you begin, you may find material for writing in the issues that concern you in day-to-day life, in memories, in conflicts that you need to work through, or in letters that you need to write but not send. Writing gives thoughts and emotions recognition when you've been uncomfortable acknowledging them, solidity when you've been confused. It allows you to read your own words, perhaps finding a new perspective from that distance. Over time, it provides a record of your journey, the story of your growth as you move through your life.

1. Assessment

We begin with an examination of where you are right now. Start your journal with the date and time on a clean page and begin to record an assessment of where you are right now. Make it more of a scientific survey than a judgment of your faults and virtues. Pretend you are assessing the "control group." Though we will most often work the chakras from bottom to top, begin this time with the spiritual aspects of your life.

Spiritual

• What is your basic form of spirituality? (Answers can be anything from the naming of a major religion to something like "walking in the park.") If you don't have any form of spirituality in your life, do you feel a lack or are you content? Do you think of spirituality as a waste of time?

• Is your form of spirituality inherited (i.e. your parent's religion) or self-chosen (or both)? If self-chosen, what events led to this choosing?

• How satisfied are you with the spiritual aspect of your life?

• What portion of your life is spent in the practice of your spirituality? Would you like this to be more or less?

Journal Exercises

- What goals would you like to set for yourself spiritually, if any? Is there spiritual programming from a childhood religion that you would like to recover or remove?

Mental

- What portion of your life is spent in mental activities (reading, writing, thinking, reasoning, solving problems, daydreaming)? Would you like it to be more or less?

- How mentally stimulating is your work? Your friendships? Your home life?

- How many books do you read in a month? How many hours of TV or other entertainment?

- Are you satisfied and confident with your mental abilities?

- Are you satisfied with your level of education?

- What is your favorite mental activity and what do you get out of it?

Emotional

- Over the course of a month, what emotional states do you spend the most time in (depression, elation, fear, joy, etc.)?

- How emotionally fulfilling do you find your life, your relationships, your work?

- What goals would you choose for yourself emotionally (i.e. to feel more confident, less angry, more passionate, more patient)?

Physical

- Take time now to feel your body. Where is it chronically tense, numb, painful? Where does it feel good, full of energy and life, or pleasure? Go into yourself deeply, exploring without judgment. Write down the places in your body that come to your attention, and what you feel there—both the good and the bad.

• As a whole, how do you feel about your body? Do you pay attention to it? Are you happy with the way it feels and behaves? Is it pleasurable to be in your body? Does your body feel like excess baggage you must carry around? Do you have chronic pain, or addictive disorders?

• How much time in each week do you give to your body (working out, getting a massage, going for a walk, making love, etc.)?

• What are your goals for your body (teeth fixed, new clothes, weight loss or gain, etc.)?

2. Chakra Body Map

On a large piece of paper draw an outline of your body. Don't worry about whether it is artistic or perfect. Color in the figure with crayons or colored pencils, letting the colors represent how that part of you feels. Let the colors flow outside of your body where you feel most free, show the blocks where you experience them with dark or angular shapes. Ask yourself how connected you feel with your ground, with the earth. How connected with spirit? How connected is your heart? Try not to overly intellectualize but to feel it. Acknowledge your feelings without judging yourself against any imagined standard of what you are supposed to feel like. (We will do the exercise again later from a different perspective.) When your picture is complete, look at it as a whole. What impressions does it give you? How do you feel about what you are looking at? Do you feel compassion, judgment, attraction, sorrow, satisfaction?

3. Rights

Refer to the description of the seven rights on page 17. For each right ask yourself: How was this right infringed upon in your life? How fully have your reclaimed this right?

The purpose of these questions is to give you a starting point, an assessment. After working through all seven chakras, you may wish to go back and read all this in your journal and compare it to how you feel at that time. Only then can you really see if you have changed.

Resources

Books

Beck, Renee & Metrick, Sydney Barbara. *The Art of Ritual*. Celestial Arts.

Bloom, William. *Sacred Times: A New Approach to Festivals*. Findhorn Press.

Cahill, Sedonia. *Ceremonial Circles*. Harper.

Judith, Anodea, *Wheels of Life: A User's Guide to the Chakra System*. Llewellyn.

Paladin, Lynda S. *Ceremonies for Change*. Stillpoint Publishing.

Chakra One
Earth

Getting Started

Where Are You Now?

Before reading the chapter or starting the exercises, take some time to explore your first chakra issues. The following words are key concepts. Look at each word and meditate on it for a few moments. In your journal, write whatever thoughts or images come to mind related to that concept.

Survival	*Home*
Earth	*Family*
Grounding	*Roots*
Matter	*Discipline*
Body	*Foundation*
Physical plane	*Stillness*

This chakra involves the feet, legs, base of spine and large intestine. How do you feel about these areas of your body? Are there any difficulties you've had in these areas at any time during your life?

Altar Arrangement

For the first chakra you will want your altar to represent the element Earth and feature symbols of personal areas of interest. If you have one place in your house that you can maintain as your altar, use that and change its features as you move through the chakras. Otherwise, you might want to put a first chakra altar in your office or place of business, your kitchen, your garden, or a special place outside that could be a permanent Earth altar. Obviously, having an altar outside limits the types of things you could put on it, so you might want to have a place inside as well.

For an indoor altar, cover the top with a red cloth or, if you prefer the natural surface of wood or stone, feature red in the objects upon it. This can include a red candle to light during your meditations, a vase of red flowers, a red or earthen ceramic plate, or other object that you feel connects you to the first chakra concepts you especially want to work on.

You may wish to add special crystals or stones you have collected, attractive pieces of wood, small potted plants, or photographs of outdoor scenes that you find particularly potent with earth energies.

If you like the idea of working with Hindu or other deities, arrange statues or pictures among the other objects. Lakshmi, the Hindu goddess of wealth, enjoys flowers, perfume and the color red. Pictures of her can be obtained inexpensively at most Indian import stores. Another particularly appropriate deity is Ganesha, the elephant headed god, remover of obstacles, who is often invoked at the start of new ventures.

The purpose of an altar is to remind yourself of the conceptual realm you have chosen to focus upon. Refer to the list of key concepts and the table of correspondences and see how you might symbolize any of the items listed. If family is a focus for you, a picture of your family could go on the altar. If money is an issue, you might want to place your checkbook there each night. If it is your physical health, perhaps a picture of your body or a mirror.

Overall, you should like the way your altar looks when you are finished. It should be a pleasing reminder to connect with the earth, with yourself, and with the things you choose to work on during this period.

Correspondences	
Sanskrit name	Muladhara
Meaning	Root
Location	Base of spine, coccygeal plexus, legs, feet, large intestine
Element	Earth
Main Issue	Survival
Goals	Stability, grounding, prosperity, right livelihood, physical health
Malfunction	Obesity, hemorrhoids, constipation, sciatica, eating disorders, knee troubles, bone disorders, frequent illness in general, frequent fears, inability to focus, "spaciness," inability to be still
Color	Red
Planet	Saturn
Foods	Protein, meats
Right	To Have
Stones	Garnet, hematite, bloodstone, lodestone
Animals	Elephant, ox, bull
Operating principle	Gravity
Yoga Path	Hatha Yoga
Archetype	Earth Mother

Sharing the Experience

"My name is Susan and I never dreamed the first chakra would be so difficult. I thought I would just breeze through it and be ready for the next six levels. But I found that everything this month tried to be unstable—my car broke down, my landlord said that he might sell the house I live in, I got a cold that put me to bed, and I over-drew my checking account. But through it all, I have a better understanding of the importance of the first chakra, because whenever these things happened, I felt totally preoccupied with them and couldn't do anything else."

•

"My name's Bob and I, too, got this cold that is going around. But it made me slow down, take a rest, institute changes in my diet, and pay attention to my body. So for me, it was really a grounding experience. I didn't get anything done around the house, though I did get in touch with how much there is to be done."

"My name is Cheryl, and I'm going through a lot around my job right now. My boss is constantly in survival mode, and is never sure from week to week whether she can pay me on time. At the beginning of the month she was ten days late and I had to borrow money to pay my rent. She paid me later, but it makes me insecure to go through this, and it affects everything else I am doing. I tried to just stay with the grounding exercises and meditations, and they helped keep me centered, but I still feel unsure and angry."

•

"I'm Richard, and I got in touch with a lot of fear. I grew up in Europe during World War II, and remember the sounds of the bombs, the shortage of food, and the times my parents sent me to stay with other relatives for long periods of time to keep me out of harm's way. Back then it felt like abandonment, and though I don't think about it much anymore, I have come to realize just how much it affected my sense of security and my ability to ground. I have a lot of first chakra issues I need to work on, and found the grounding exercises particularly difficult to do, but helpful when I did work on them. There was a very strong tendency to avoid them, however, which I guess is saying something."

Understanding the Concept

Our long climb upward through the individual chakras begins with the first chakra at the base of the spine. This level represents *our roots, our foundation, our bodies,* and *our survival.* Our purpose here is to build a strong foundation that will support all our subsequent work, and to strengthen that foundation through roots that are solid and deep, a body that is healthy and strong, and stability in our livelihood. These are not easy tasks and many people find the first chakra the most challenging of all the chakras.

The name of the first chakra is *Muladhara,* which literally means root. In order to grow tall and sturdy, a plant needs strong roots nestled deep in the rich soil of earth. Just as roots grow downward, our first chakra experience is one of moving energy and attention *downward* in our bodies—*down* to the base of our spine, *down* to the legs and feet, *down* into our guts, *down* into our past, our ancestral roots. As we move downward, we move into the associated element of the first chakra, which is *earth.*

The tasks of this chakra involve getting in touch with the earth, establishing a good sense of grounding, taking care of our survival needs, and taking care of the body. When there is damage to the chakra, these things become monumental tasks. When the chakra is healthy and balanced they become rudimentary tasks, maintenance programs that run smoothly and provide the stability needed to accomplish other things.

Chakra One represents the heaviest and densest forms of matter, and operates along the principles of gravity. Gravity is the process whereby a substance pulls other bits of matter towards itself. In a body the size of the earth, we experience this as a downward pull. From a larger perspective, however, we see that gravity draws matter towards the center of the earth from all sides. Gravity, in terms of the first chakra, can be seen as the *inward pull of the center.*

Manifestation

Our downward path of manifestation ends at the first chakra and indeed manifestation is what this chakra is all about. Manifestation is a process of pulling things together in one place. If I choose to manifest dinner, I take food from the store, from the garden, from the cupboard and refrigerator and bring it together in one place. In manifesting a book, information is taken from many sources and brought together to become one source with its own central theme. Certainly the ability to survive and prosper depends on our ability to manifest what we need.

Matter in the first chakra exists in its most solid and specific form. It has edges and boundaries, size, shape and purpose. To bring our thoughts and desires into manifestation, we need to be very specific about what we want to manifest. We don't, for example, just go out and build a house. We make specific plans about size, shape, style, cost estimation, location and timing. To manifest a good dinner, we don't just throw food together, but follow very specific patterns of ingredients, measurement and cooking time. Many people have difficulty focusing attention long enough to work out the specific nuts and bolts of a situation. As a result, the situation recurs again and again. Generalizing is for the upper chakras, but not for the building of our foundation.

Early Development

The development of the first chakra occurs throughout one's life, but most intensely during the first year of life. Prenatal circumstances such as what vitamins or chemicals the mother takes during pregnancy, how she feels about giving birth, how tight the womb is, and, of course, the birth process itself, all have an effect on the first chakra. Traumatic birth makes for difficult entry into our physical bodies, and therefore the first chakra. Separation from the mother directly after birth, as occurs with incubator babies or simply the barbaric standard practices of some hospitals that rip the child away and take him to a bright and noisy nursery, also create initial damage to the first chakra. With practices such as these considered normal, it is no wonder we have a culture so out of touch with its ground and with the Earth!

During this stage of life, the consciousness of the newborn is centered primarily around the instincts of survival. Hunger, warmth, comfort, and a sense of our existence being welcomed set the stage for a healthy and fulfilled first chakra. According to the scheme of developmental stages set forth by Erik Erikson, the issue of trust versus mistrust is determined at this time. Successful attendance to survival needs during infancy creates a feeling of trust in the world. This is the time when we want the spirit to come solidly into the body. The child learns that a body well-fed, loved and cared for is pleasant to live in, as is the world around it. She learns that the expression of her needs can result in manifestation which creates a basis for the ability to manifest later in life.

Trauma, abandonment, physical abuse, hardship, hunger, or physical difficulties damage the first chakra. Our basic survival program is then built on mistrust. Pain and trauma teach us to override our body's needs, to ignore them, sublimate them. Energetically, the child pulls his energy upward in his body, away from the roots. The child is pulled up out of his ground, the very thing that is developing at that stage. Pulling a plant up by its roots does not encourage it to grow.

To heal from traumas in the first chakra involves going back to our "inner infant" and recreating the sense of welcoming, honoring and bonding that should have occurred. This may take the help of a friend or therapist. John Bradshaw, in his book *Homecoming*, offers a list of affirmations to read as healing salve for difficulty at this age. Here are some examples from his book, plus some we've added:

Welcome to the world, I've been waiting for you.
I'm so glad you're here.
I've prepared a special place for you.
It is very safe here.
All your needs will be provided.
You have a wonderful body.
You are absolutely unique and necessary.

It may take many sessions of returning to this age and reaffirming your right to be here before these affirmations take effect. It may be necessary to create a fantasy of an "ideal Mommy," who can provide the right support. The important thing to receive from this fantasy is the feeling of a sense of trust in the world—of trust in the Earth to support us, and trust in ourselves to manifest what we need to survive. It is the feeling of trust that creates a secure first chakra.

The Body

Our physical universe begins with our body. It is the only physical certainty in our lives from birth to death, and we only get one. We cannot stress enough the importance of the body in the first chakra and in the whole chakra system. It is the foundation upon which everything else begins and ends. Our body is the home for our spirit. It is the physical manifestation of all that happens to us, the hardware in which all our programs run.

First chakra work focuses on the body, beginning with awareness. We focus on health, diet, fitness, exercise, and physical interactions with the world. We pay attention to how we feel about our body, and to how we feel in our body. Do we feel awake and alive? Do we feel sluggish and heavy?

Mastering the first chakra involves gaining an understanding and healing of our own bodies, and of the part they play in our overall state of consciousness and interaction with the world around us. This is no easy task. For some it may be the crux of their work, requiring attention and focus greater than that of any other chakra. For others, the body may be healthy, but taken for granted, and a great source of information and pleasure is then absent from our consciousness.

Healing the body is an exciting journey of reclamation. With it comes a healing of all the chakras.

Home and Finance

The issue of home is also related to the first chakra. Attention to the physical space that comprises our home, as well as the emotional sense of home, is part of the work of fortifying our foundation. If our childhood home was not a pleasant place, or if there were frequent moves that hindered our sense of stability, we need to rewrite our program about how to create a nurturing and stable home for ourselves. This can be done by giving special time and focus to our current home, keeping it clean, redecorating, or planting a garden. (See "Putting It Into Practice" at end of chapter).

Our larger home is the Earth, and in the first chakra we can also look at our care for the planet as the home for us all. Our personal home is our personal piece of the Earth. The concept of caring for our home engenders the concept of caring for the Earth—our little piece that is specifically entrusted to us.

Other work in chakra one involves attendance to the details of our mundane reality. Money, food, housing, sleep, and cleaning are aspects of our daily lives that are rudimentary subroutines of our survival programs. Our sense of prosperity has to do with our right to have, our innate sense of value, the socioeconomic conditions of our childhood, and our ability to engage with the mundane world in a grounded and effective way.

Excess and Deficiency

First chakra blockages can manifest as either excess or deficiency. A deficient first chakra is not developed enough to provide adequate support, containment, or solidity for the needs of the individual. This is due to issues in early development, as mentioned earlier.

Manifestations of first chakra deficiency are many. Chief among them are a tendency toward frequent fear, a reaction to perceived threats to our survival which may carry over even when there is no current threat. Since the solidity of the first chakra provides containment, a deficient chakra leaves us with poor boundaries. This may appear as difficulties in saying no, prolonging gratification, saving money, or working with adequate self-discipline to achieve a goal. The first chakra also provides the ability to focus on a specific task, so a deficiency shows up as a tendency to feel spacey, vague, or scattered, or unable to stick with a task long enough to complete it. And lastly, a deficient first chakra makes it difficult to be fully in the body, perhaps causing health problems or simply a sense of being out of touch with the physical world. As the foundation for the ability to provide for ourselves, deficiency can leave us with a constantly troubled financial situation, an experience of "always being in survival."

Excesses in the first chakra are seen in the pattern of clinging to security. Hoarding possessions, fear of change, needing to ground through physical weight are all examples of needing excess in the first chakra in order to feel normal.

It is important to realize that both of these conditions result from damage to the first chakra. Excess and deficiency are merely different ways to cope with the imbalance. Deficiency is an avoidance response to first chakra issues, while excess is an overcompensation.

First chakra work is complex in our society. It takes time to get grounded, to get all our affairs in order, to get our bodies healthy, and our means of support running smoothly. Some people spend a whole lifetime at it. It is not a job that is ever done—we eat and sleep nearly every day. The real challenge and resolution of the first chakra is to make this work of grounding a well-integrated part of our everyday life.

Working with Movement

The movements of the first chakra provide us with grounding and bring awareness to the body and its relationship with the earth via gravity. Many of the specific movements will stimulate the area of the body where muladhara waits patiently for energy to flow through it. We begin this movement of energy through the feet, legs, and sacrum area, these being a conduit for earth's energy as it enters the body. The body parts that are generally in contact with the earth become focus points for our movement here—feet (as we stand), buttocks (as we sit), back (as we lie down). We will be stretching and releasing muscles which keep the first chakra constrained.

As you do these exercises, notice where you feel held back, where the tight places are. Breathe into these areas as you stretch, imagining your breath bringing life and energy to cells and muscle tissue that have been isolated from that flow. Pay attention to the strength involved in performing the practice. Notice the contraction of muscles as they work to create the movement or solidity of each exercise.

Muladhara deals with physical world phenomena, and working with the body in any way is an important part of acquainting yourself with the state of your first chakra. This is your opportunity to discover how steady and stable you are on your feet, how comfortable in your steps on the earth, how balanced as you interact with your physical surroundings.

Pelvis Breathing

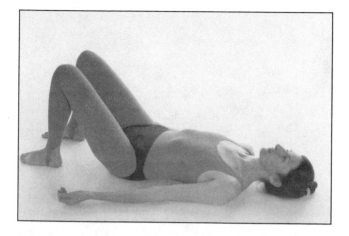

1 Begin lying down on your back. Pull your knees up so that your feet are on the ground as wide apart as your hips. As you breathe in, expand your diaphragm, pushing your abdomen out slightly. As you release each breath, allow your abdomen to empty out.

2 Taking this movement further, create a space under the small of your back as you breathe in.

3 Then press it down to the floor as you breathe out. This does not need to be a large movement, just an expansion of the natural movement of your breath. As you continue to breathe your lower back into and away from the floor, keep the rest of your body as relaxed as possible. You should notice a slight movement of your torso and head in the direction of your head as you breathe out and back down as you breathe in. This reflects the length of your spine in relation to the floor as the curve in your lower back is alternately straightened and arched.

While breathing in this controlled fashion, imagine that the earth is breathing through your body—you become the earth breathing. Feel yourself expanding and then sinking down into earth with each cycle of breath, connecting this vital life-sustaining function with the life of the earth.

Bridge

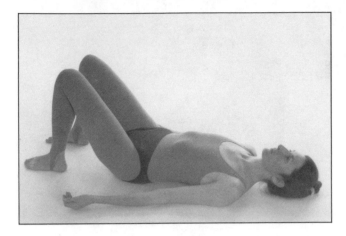

1 This movement strengthens and stimulates the first chakra. Begin with a deep breath in and as you begin to breathe out, press your lower back into the floor as you did for the Pelvis breath.

3 If this feels comfortable and you want to go further, continue pressing your groin and thighs upward toward the ceiling, contracting the muscles in your buttocks to protect your lower back. You may stay in your final position for a few moments, but only for as long as you can continue to press infinitesimally upwards.

2 Continue to breathe out as you follow the inclination of your buttocks to leave the floor by pressing upwards, starting with your lower thigh and moving up towards your groin and pelvis. Imagine that there is a rope attached to your tailbone that is pulling between your legs and up towards the ceiling, rolling you off the floor by tilting your pelvis upwards first and then moving up your spine vertebrae by vertebrae. If you have any difficulties with your back, or if this feels like all you can handle at this point, stay at the position shown above.

This

Not This

Bridge (continued)

4 When you feel yourself unable to be actively working in the pose, come back down slowly by rolling your spine into the floor from the top down, leaving your tailbone for last. Rest in this position and feel the reconnection of your first chakra with the earth.

Leg Folding

1 Pull both legs in toward your chest with knees bent while keeping the lower back and top of the buttocks on the ground. Feel the connection of your first chakra with the earth beneath you.

2 Continue to be aware of this connection as you stretch one leg out along the floor. Hold this pose for a moment and then switch legs. Alternate legs several times, then let both legs stretch out and rest, paying attention to the sensations in your body, particularly at the first chakra.

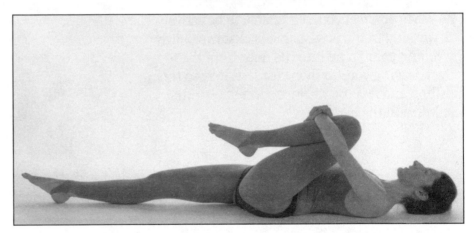

Although this exercise focuses on the movement of the legs, there is a great deal of activity occurring at the root chakra, primarily around the sacrum area. As you are performing the leg movements, be aware of the more subtle movements at the base of your spine and visualize the first chakra extending from there down through your legs.

Rolling

1 Stretch your arms above your head, feeling the length of your body along the floor. Bend your right knee enough to allow you to press your right foot into the ground as you imagine a rope attached to your right front hip bone pulling the right side of your body off the floor and over to your left side, using the push of your right foot on the ground to assist the movement. Your right hip bone leads you while the rest of your body follows passively along, allowing you to experience a slight twist in your spine as you roll over onto your belly.

2 Continue the roll from your belly by reaching with your left arm behind you and across your body, pulling you onto your right side and then over onto your back, the hips and legs following along last. Continue rolling in the same direction for as long as the floor space allows, then reverse directions and roll back. If you plan to go on to the next segment of the Muladhara movement sequence, finish on your belly.

In this exercise, be aware of gravity's pull on your body. Notice your relationship with the ground as different areas of your body sink into it during your rolling. Feel your weight as you allow it to pull you down into the floor on each roll. This is an exercise in surrendering, allowing an ease in your movements as you include your entire body in a dance with the floor.

Locust

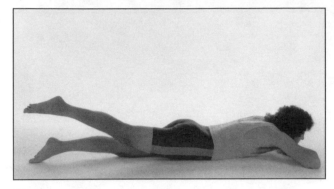

This

Not This

1 Place your arms in a comfortable position. Lengthen your right leg along the floor, contracting the front of the thigh to straighten the leg and reaching through your foot, as if you were sending energy down your leg from your sacrum. Maintain this position as you lift the leg off the floor, while keeping the right front hip bone pressing into or towards the floor. Be careful not to lift the right front hip bone. Lower the leg back down to the floor and release the muscles, feeling the sensations in your leg and first chakra area. Repeat with the left leg. Alternate legs, resting briefly between each lift to experience the energy moving in your body. This movement stimulates the first chakra and strengthens the muscles of that area.

2 When you have worked with this movement for long enough to accustom your body to the muscular work and alignment necessary, then you can build on the strength you have established and lift both legs at once. Place arms and hands under your hips or pelvis and lift both legs off the ground at once, maintaining your awareness of the sacrum area as you lift and when you release and relax.

Child's Pose

Lying face down, bring your hands to the floor on either side of your shoulders and press, lifting yourself onto your hands and knees and then lowering your torso onto your legs. You can extend your arms forward or tuck them alongside your torso. This might also be called the Rock pose, as your body curls itself into a solid, earthy mass.

Child's Pose is a rest position that is especially beneficial after practicing backbends (like the Locust leg lifts). You may also use this pose to increase awareness and energy in your back. We often think about breathing as expanding our bodies towards the front, but the lungs should expand to the sides and back as well. In Child's Pose, breathe into your back, feeling the opening and releasing with each breath. Imagine each breath moving down your spine to the sacrum, enlivening the root chakra area.

If you have difficulty with this pose, place a rolled up towel or blanket between your feet and your buttocks. If your head does not reach the floor, you may benefit from a cushion under your head. If your ankles are uncomfortable, place a narrow rolled towel under them. Experiment with these aids until you find a way to be reasonably comfortable in the pose.

Squat

1 From Child's Pose, place your hands near your knees, tuck your toes under, and transfer your weight to your feet. Feet should be about hip width apart (about one foot apart). Be aware of the solid ground under your hands, and position your metatarsals firmly and evenly in preparation for shifting your weight back onto your feet. The feet and lower leg stretch as you practice Squat, and these areas are very much a part of the first chakra, as they are the primary connection of our bodies with the earth.

2 Balance on the metatarsal or, if you can, sink your weight back onto the entire foot. Maintain this pose, bringing your awareness to the opening in the sacrum area and in the space between your genitals and your anus. Relax into this pose, allowing the weight of your body to pull your heels down towards the ground.

This position is important, as you are about to transfer the connection that your entire body has had with the floor to a smaller section of the body—your feet. In the Squat, your hands are used as well as the feet to solidify your connection with the ground before you make the full transition to your feet.

Spinal Roll

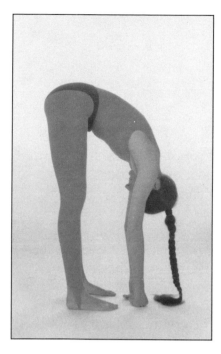  

1 From the Squat, sink your weight into your heels and begin to straighten your legs (do not completely straighten them yet if you have lower back problems). Allow your upper body to hang forward from the tailbone, releasing the muscles in your neck so that your head can hang heavy.

2 When you've straightened your knees as far as feels comfortable, begin to roll up your spine, as if you were placing each vertebrae on top of the one beneath it.

3 As you come up to the shoulders, let them drop down, as if the shoulder blades were sliding down your back, then lift the head on your lengthened neck. Bring your awareness from your head down through your torso and legs through your feet and into the ground, feeling gravity connecting and rooting you to earth at the same time that you feel yourself lifting and growing out of the earth.

Balancing

Standing on both feet, bring your awareness to how you distribute weight on your feet. Are you standing on your heels? Your toes? One foot more than the other? Experiment with this, rolling back and forth and side to side on your feet, noticing where you feel comfortable, where you feel off balance.

Let one foot carefully lift just barely off the floor, maintaining your balance. If you start to lose the balance bring the foot closer to the floor or even touch it lightly to the ground, find your center and balance again, and lift from this center, going only as high as your balance allows. This is not about how high you can lift your leg, but rather how stable your grounding on one leg can be. Shift slowly from one leg to the other in this manner, working into a slow, deliberate walk. Maintain your sense of balance in all phases of this walking, working with gravity and your weight on the ground to keep yourself steady and stable.

The Dance

The dance of *muladhara* begins with the state your body is in whenever you begin the dance. This means that if there are aches and pains, tightness, injuries, or vulnerable areas, they are included in the dance. The idea is not to imagine some ideal and perfect set of movements for the first chakra and then attempt to force your body into them. Instead, we are opening the body to the energy of the first chakra and seeing what it does when that energy enters and begins to move with your body. Follow the movements that come naturally at that point, experiencing and observing the sensations.

Begin your dance from whatever position brings you most into your root chakra. This may be one of the positions we've outlined for you here, but it could also be a position that your body goes to naturally when you think about grounding yourself. You might try beginning the dance from different positions to see how the energy works for you. You may eventually find yourself coming back to one pose again and again for periods of time. This may or may not change later. Play music that evokes first chakra energy for you, either one of the tapes we've listed, or something you've found yourself.

Start by sinking your weight down into the ground, growing roots into the soil beneath you. As you breathe, imagine that you are the earth, breathing in through your body and down into the bowels of the earth. Follow the breath in and out with this image, then allow that breath to move as your body expands and releases. The movements take on a life of their own through your muscles and bones, using the energy of your breath to fuel the dance. Let the music and gravity's pull on your body combine with your breathing to become a dance of earth, root energy.

First chakra dances sometimes include slow, ponderous, heavy movements, perhaps with a plodding quality that expresses the sense of inertia and the solidity of earth. You might find yourself making small, subtle movements, evoking the stability that we associate with earth. Earth has it's earthquakes, too, and your movements may express that large, rumbling, shake-up. Perhaps you will dance the large sweeping landscape of mountains and meadows, or let your movements reflect the rootedness of a huge tree as its branches are moved by the forces of air. Let the images of earth that inspire your vision of the first chakra inspire your body's movements as well, letting your dance grow and change over time as your explorations in this chakra deepen your understanding of what it means to you. If there are stuck places in this chakra, you might imagine where these appear in your body, or what movement form they take, and let a dance emerge out of the struggle to break through.

Bioenergetic Movement

Bioenergetics is a branch of psychotherapy that focuses on releasing blocked energy patterns in the body. Emotional trauma results in the formation of "character armor," a chronic pattern of holding tension in our muscles and organs that affects, eventually, our posture, our health, and our ability to cope or create in the world.

One of the most fundamental principles in bioenergetics is the concept of grounding. Grounding is a state of dynamic contact with the earth made through our bodies, especially the legs and feet. It is rather amazing in our sophisticated culture that no matter how tall we are, how strong, or how powerful, that if someone were to push against us while standing, we can only resist them by grabbing on to the earth with our feet. Most of the time, those few square inches on the soles of the feet are the only parts of our bodies that have contact with anything solid and immovable. If our connection with the bottom of our feet is tenuous, we have no place from which to resist forces that push us "off our ground." We become, in effect, pushovers. We have seen huge men who could be pushed off balance with the slightest pressure, and tiny women who were immovable—all from their individual ability to ground through their feet.

The following exercise is a simple grounding exercise that can be done every day. It will increase the charge of excitation in the legs and feet, and consequently feed energy into the first chakra. It can be done to *stimulate* the first chakra, but is *not* recommended for calming. It should be done a little at a time, developing slowly the ability to tolerate charge. It is possible, in some cases, to become overcharged through this exercise. Some people experience this as excitement, and others as anxiety. If you become anxious or shaky through this exercise, it is because you are pushing blocked energy towards release. Take a walk or do some vigorous exercise, or find the help of a friend or therapist to facilitate its release.

Bioenergetic Movement: The Elephant

Part 1

Stand relaxed, with feet about shoulder width apart, toes parallel or turned slightly inward. Knees are slightly bent at all times, the belly is loose (no holding your stomach in here), the jaw is loose so that you can breathe through your mouth. (Breathing through the mouth is better for lower chakra work, the nose is better for the upper chakras.) Take a moment to bounce and let a little sound out, loosening your muscles as much as possible.

Slowly let your head come forward to your chest, and then slowly follow with the rest of your spine until you are hanging in a rag doll position, fingertips gently touching the floor, knees slightly bent. This is Position 1. Feel your legs under you. Now slowly breathe in while bending your knees until your thighs are almost parallel to the floor if you can, moving into Position 2. If this is difficult, bend them as much as you can.

When your breath is full, exhale slowly and push your feet into the floor, such that your legs straighten enough to return to position 1. *Never straighten your knees completely*. It locks the knees and cuts off the circuit we are trying to stimulate. Continue to breathe and move from Position 1 to 2, inhaling as you bend, exhaling as you straighten. Within a short time you will become very aware of your thighs. They may shake or vibrate, or they may simply burn. It is a sign that you are doing it right! Now you are ready for part 2!

Position 1

Position 2

The Elephant (continued)

Part 2

Before your thighs become totally exhausted, begin to straighten your upper body a little bit each time you push into the floor. Think of yourself as an empty water balloon, that fills bit by bit and stands up as it becomes full. Each push brings energy into your body, and as your body fills it becomes upright, still with the knees slightly bent.

When you get to the upright position, continue to inhale while bending your knees, and breathe out pushing into the floor. Think of it as pushing the floor away from you rather than moving your torso upward. Push *through* your legs rather than pushing *with* your legs. Check to see if your feet are still parallel and shoulder width apart with the knees bent out over the toes. If you can see your feet, you should be able to see your big toe just inside your kneecap when you look down.

This exercise will also produce a trembling in the legs. Think of this trembling as a new charge of energy coming through areas that have been previously blocked or otherwise understimulated. Try to relax and enjoy the trembling. Exaggerate the feeling with your legs and allow the energy to move upward into the rest of your body if it is ready to do so.

Bioenergetic Movement: Legs Against the Wall

Lay on your back on a non-slippery surface, with your feet against a solid wall. Position yourself so that your thighs are perpendicular to the floor, and your calves are parallel. Simply push down into your feet, pushing into the wall, again trying to push *through* your legs, rather than simply tightening all the muscles. Push for a bit and then relax, and see how your body feels, then push again, alternating until you feel that your legs are awake, alive, and energized.

The following exercises establish the concept of ground in the face of adversity.

Partner Work: Earth Skiing

Stand opposite your partner, feet shoulder width apart, with your toes about two feet from your partner's toes. Both of you reach forward, each grabbing on to the wrist of the other, arms crossed in front. (Note: It is important to do this on a non-slippery surface—barefoot if it is a smooth floor, or on a non-slip rug.)

With a firm hold on each other's wrists, lean back, pushing your feet into the floor. Push into your heels, as if you were water skiing. Pull back against your partner until each of you is in a position that looks like you are sitting in an invisible chair, thighs parallel to the floor, and calves perpendicular, with your backs straight. Keep your elbows straight and let your weight do the work. This position forces you to ground through your legs, and, if you are doing it right, you will feel it in your thighs.

Partner Work: Pushing

Stand opposite a partner with your feet in the grounding position, knees slightly bent, weight low in your body. Your partner assumes the same position a little less than an arm's length away.

Partner A gently pushes upon the chest, shoulders, or belly of Partner B in an attempt to push the partner off ground. Partner B pushes into her feet and stays centered. Slowly allow the pushes to get stronger and the strength of the grounding to increase. Partner B is striving to make a clear and solid energetic connection between the force from Partner A and the ground. Sustained pushes provide time to feel this connection deeply.

Switch roles.

Partner Work: Using Resistance

This is a slower exercise. Stand with feet shoulder width apart, about an arm's length from your partner. Bend your knees slightly and get a sense of your ground. Raise your hands and touch your partner's palms. This time you are not trying to push your partner; you are pushing against *each other* such that you each increase the energy running to your feet in order to stay centered. As you push against your partner, you must also push your feet into the ground. The push between you must stay balanced, of course. See how much energy you can get to run through your legs and body by using the resistance of your partner's pushing.

Partner Work: Slap Hands

The former exercise can now become a game, suitable for loosening up a new group and illustrating the principles of grounding at the same time.

Two people stand opposite each other, feet shoulder width apart, toes pointing forward, about a foot and a half from each other. Play begins by hitting against your partner's palms, trying to send them off balance as they attempt to do the same thing to you. Sounds simple?

There are three rules to this game that create more of a challenge than you might think.

1. You cannot touch any part of your partner's body, except for the palms of the hands.

2. You cannot move your feet from their position at all.

3. You can move your hands aside to dodge your partner's pushing.

If you move your hands aside and your partner slips and touches your shoulders, you win that round. If your partner pushes your hands and you have to move your feet to maintain balance, your partner wins that round.

Keep your weight low and stay centered in your own ground. Too far forward or back and you will either touch your partner or move your feet.

Partner Work: Push Me—Pull You

This is similar in principle to the above exercise, but focuses more on pulling.

Stand opposite your partner, right leg ahead, left leg behind. You and your partner touch the outsides of your right feet together and grab hands. The object is to push or pull the person off balance, using only the hands that are touching. Anyone who moves their feet loses the round. Keep your weight low!

Group Work: Rolling

All the participants lie down on the floor side by side, bodies close together, arms over their heads. The person on one end rolls herself over onto the person next to her and proceeds to roll over the human rug, going slowly and carefully, but not holding herself up. When the roller reaches the end of the line, she joins the end of the line and becomes ground for the next person to roll over. One by one, each member of the group rolls down the line of people, allowing everyone involved to experience themselves as the living, breathing ground for all their fellow group members, and also to experience with their bodies the support that is there for them in this group.

Putting It Into Practice

Listed below are real-world tasks that are related to consolidating your first chakra. Each one brings focus and attention to aspects of our lives necessary for building a solid foundation.

Body

Tend to any nagging diseases or physical discomforts that have been chronic. Get that throat culture done. Have that chronic spot in your back looked at. Get the complete physical exam you've been talking about. This may or may not involve western medicine, but does involve paying attention to symptoms in some responsible way.

Pay attention to your diet and experiment with some change. If you have never tried a vegetarian diet, here's your chance. If you haven't eaten meat in years, try it and see how it affects you now. Change your diet to lose or gain weight and to provide better nourishment, experiment with allergies, or go on a short fast (longer fasts are not good for grounding or health). You might want to keep a food journal of all that you eat for five days, and analyze it for nutritional content and balance. Look for patterns in your moods and energy levels that relate to what you eat.

Pamper yourself—give your body a treat. Get a massage, take a sauna, a dance class, a nice dinner out, or a clothes shopping trip. Let yourself get extra sleep, extra exercise, go running, hiking, dancing. Massage your feet, carefully and lovingly.

LOVE YOUR BODY!

Home

Our home is our external first chakra. It is the outer manifestation of our inner space. Look around your home and see how it reflects you. Is it a comfortable, grounding place to be? Does it nurture you to be there? Do you spend enough time there? Too much?

This is the time to do those things around the house that make it a nicer place to live. Clean out your closets, garage, or basement. Paint the bedroom, fix the back door, rearrange your kitchen cupboards, build shelves, or clean your yard. Attend to those physical chores that are part of your physical space.

Business

Business is the expression of the first chakra. What you do to attend to your business life will vary greatly, but simple things might involve: clean and reorganize your desk or files. Make a new business card. Apply for a loan or pay back a loan. Ask for a raise. Put out a new ad. Open a new branch. Hire an assistant. Invest some money.

The general idea is to improve your connection to business by giving it focused attention, and to increase its ability to provide you a solid, comfortable foundation.

Finance

Similar to business but more personal. Balance your checkbook, consolidate your accounts, do an analysis of your spending. Make a list each day of what you spend money on and draw it up as a graph, i.e. how much for food, rent, entertainment, gas, clothing, books, etc. Watch this for a month. Make a budget for yourself if appropriate.

Possessions

Consolidate your possessions. Fix that switch on your electric saw, give away old clothes, have a garage sale, buy something you've been wanting. Make a list of items you would like to have in the future and prioritize, remembering that manifestation is what the first chakra is for, and being specific is one of its methods. As you prioritize, think about what you need them for, what you can do to get them, and by when you would like to have them (such as a new car by next winter, a new home in five years, etc.).

Family

Your family of origin was your first umbilical cord to your survival. Are there contacts that you need to clean up? Your ancestors are your roots, and Muladhara means root. You might do a genealogy on your family, do a ritual to your ancestors, or contact your grandmother, and learn about your history. If your family is horribly dysfunctional, your family work might include cutting ties for awhile, or using therapy to work on family patterns.

Earth

The element of this chakra is earth. Our job here is to gain better ground through connecting with the earth. Take walks in the woods, wiggle bare toes in mud, go canvassing for an environmental cause, or write letters to Congressmen about the environment. Start a garden or work in a neighbor's garden, or transplant your house plants into larger pots. Go on a backpacking trip into the wilderness, surrounded by earth in its natural form. Go to a rock show, spend time with your crystals, or build an altar of rocks and plants. Read a geology book, or a book such as *Deep Ecology*, or *Gaia, An Atlas of Planet Management* (see Resources at the end of this chapter).

General

All of these tasks work together. To change your diet and not attempt to exercise will only give you a small benefit. To do physical work and not get a massage or give a treat to your body will make first chakra work seem hopelessly unpleasant. Working harder without spending time in the earth does not bring balance to the first chakra.

Obviously there are enough tasks listed here to keep you busy for a year. These are merely suggestions, and you can pick the ones most appropriate for your life. But try to do a couple of things from each category, so that your first chakra practice is well-rounded.

Journal Exercises

1. Examining Your Programming

Survival is the main issue of the first chakra. Programmed at a time we were too young to remember, our ideas of survival become ingrained in our nervous system, affecting our ground, our sense of contact and connection, and our ability to provide for our own needs. Few people are free of survival issues. The following questions may help you focus on your own issues around survival and physicality.

• How was your survival provided for you in the past? By whom? At what price? In what kind of atmosphere? How do you feel about those who provided for you now? How did you feel about them in the past?

• How do you exhibit trust or mistrust in the way you approach your survival needs and your ability to obtain them?

• How much honor and importance do you give to your physical body? How well do you take care of yourself?

• What is it that keeps you from wanting to be here?

• How do you interfere with the manifesting of your survival needs?

• Chakra One is the right to have—was this right inhibited in your upbringing? If so, how and by whom? What can you do to change it?

2. Being Specific

Write down something that you want to manifest. Follow it with a description that is as specific as you can possibly get. Make the specifics address the final form as well as all the steps necessary to get there.

3. The Body—Mirror Work

Find time alone with a large mirror and remove all your clothes. Stand in front of the mirror and look at your body, not from a place of judgment about its size or shape, but with an attitude of greeting. Pretend you are seeing a species for the first time, and you have no preconceptions about how bodies should look.

Journal Exercises

This is you. This is the statement your spirit is making at this time. Look at the details of this statement with compassion, pleasure or amusement, but not criticism. If your chest caves in, just feel what it's like to be depressed in that area rather than judge. If you like your chest, allow yourself to feel pleasure in that.

Look at the places that are hard or armored. Touch them. Talk to them. Ask them what they might be afraid of. Notice what chakra areas are most armored. For instance, neck and shoulder tightness relates to the throat chakra. Legs relate to chakra one, and chest to chakra four. Be gentle with yourself there. Give yourself permission to relax.

Look at the places where weight accumulates. Again, don't criticize! Touch these places gently. Feel yourself extending out to their edges. Feel your need to have this protection, to be this size. Allow yourself to let your belly relax, your buttocks release, your shoulders hang the way they feel most comfortable. Allow your energy to fill all your flesh, finding beauty in its unique curves and folds.

Most people hate their fat, and therefore take their life energy away from it. It becomes a "dead weight" with no life force in it. It must be claimed to be changed. When you can allow it to be part of yourself, then it can be incorporated into your body as a whole and change along with the rest of you.

Close your eyes and let your body stand the way it feels best from inside, regardless of how it might look from outside. Then open your eyes and regard it, again looking for the statement it is making. If you had to put that statement in one sentence, starting with "I," what would it be? (eg. I'm lonely, I'm scared, I'm powerful, I'm sexy, I'm guarded, I'm angry). Say it aloud with your eyes shut and then again to your reflection. How does it feel to accept the statement your body is making? Say it several times, say it with the emotion you are stating. Say it angrily if you are angry, sadly if you are sad. Let your body make movements that reflect the statement. Shake your fists if you are angry. Tighten your shoulders if you are scared. Sensuously move your hips if you say "I am sexy." How does your body respond?

Next, allow yourself to put on the armor you wear for the world. Pull your shoulders back, tuck your belly in, raise your head high, put on your smiling face, and say "Hello" to your reflection. What happens to your body? What happens to its energy? How do you feel?" How different is it from a few moments ago? Go back and forth a few times between these two states. In a normal day we do this all the time—relaxing when alone, tightening up when others are watching.

Relax again and tell your body it's OK to let go of the form that is "for others." Let it make its own statement.

Next, crawl under the covers to keep warm and get out your journal. Spend a few moments writing down your feelings and impressions from the previous exercise. Write the your core statement several times and see what comes up for you. Draw a simplified picture of your body—impressionist style. Write down what you most want to change, and where you think the trait came from. Write down what you like. Express what you feel.

Take a hot bath as a reward, or if you're still going strong, continue with the next exercise.

4. Body Statements

Find a comfortable place to relax where you won't be disturbed. Get out your journal and start a new page. (This can be also be done in pairs, with one person taking notes for the other.)

Relax your body with your eyes shut and just feel it. Then, beginning with your feet, imagine that you are your feet. You are their experience, their personality. Say to yourself, "I am my feet and I…" ending the sentence with a metaphoric statement of their experience. Typical examples might be, "I am my feet and I never get to rest," or "I carry all the weight in this system," or "I am totally ignored." In your journal write "feet" in the margin, and write the statement of the experience directly opposite.

Go on to your ankles, then calves, knees, thighs, buttocks, hips, genitals, belly, low back, stomach, mid back, chest, breasts, shoulders, arms, neck, face, mouth, lips, eyes, ears, head. Do the same things for each—pretending that you are these parts—giving them a voice and writing it down. Do not edit or censor any of what comes to you. Do, however, try to stick to experiential statements rather than judgmental ones, such as "I am the stomach and I need to be big enough to nourish my person," rather than "I am the stomach and I'm too fat." If the latter statement is the strongest one then go ahead and write it down, and simply notice the places where the judgment is stronger than the experience.

When you finish, read back over your statements, covering the margin and leaving out the naming of body parts. Let them run together and read them as a statement about you.

Here's a small example from an actual transcription:

> *Feet:*   *I am tired and sore. I feel ignored.*
>
> *Ankles:*   *I don't ever think of myself. I'm hardly here.*

Journal Exercises

Calves: *I want to run and play. I'm tight and weighed down. I want to be free.*

Knees: *I feel old and creaky. I don't bend very easily.*

Thighs: *I feel dull and slow. It's not much fun carrying all this weight. I want some fun.*

Hips: *I feel solid and strong. I'd like to move more though.*

Buttocks: *I just get sat on and left behind. I want to dance more, get noticed.*

Genitals: *I feel lonely. I want someone to visit me. Sometimes I feel scared, but sometimes I feel excited.*

Once you have been through the whole body you will see patterns emerging. You may find your lower body has very little to say and your upper body says a lot. Or that your lower body carries all your pain while the upper body feels great. You may find it difficult to make "feeling" statements, or discover that each body part wants to write long paragraphs. All these points bring you information about your body's experience in the world.

Reassessment

• What have you learned about yourself as you've worked through the activities for the first chakra?

• What areas of this chakra do you still need to work on? How will you do that?

• What areas of this chakra do you feel pleased with? How can you utilize these strengths?

• On a scale of 1 - 10, how much have you reclaimed your right to have?

Entering Sacred Space

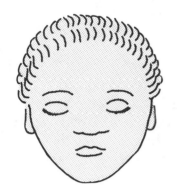

Tree of Life Meditation

Stand quietly, eyes closed, and plant yourself firmly on your two feet. Feel them supporting you, and find a comfortable center of balance, aligning your chakras in a vertical column. Imagine that your torso is the trunk of a tree, solid and straight, ready to sink its roots deep into the earth.

Take a breath in as you bend your knees and release the breath as you push your feet into the ground, pushing through your legs. As you push into the ground, imagine yourself as a tree pushing your roots into the fertile soil, pushing them out of your trunk, down into the topsoil, feeling for nutrients, water, stability. Push those roots DOWN through the soil, into the solid packed earth below, into the bedrock, breaking through the solid rock, probing deeper, growing stronger, always pushing down, deep into Mother Earth. Continue to breathe and bend your knees, exhaling and pushing even deeper, probing for the hot, red liquid core of the earth, the center of all that lies below, feeling the heat feeding into your roots, energizing them, enlivening them, and filling them so that the hot, molten core of the earth begins to rise through your roots.

Feel it rising up through the layers of the earth, the roots gathering strength, becoming more alive, filling and pouring upward through the hard layers of bedrock, the packed dark layers of old soil, into the lighter, more nutritious topsoil, pouring into your feet and rising up your legs. Bend your knees and feel it energizing your knees and your thighs with each movement, flowing upward into your base chakra, filling it with the red of the molten core. Feel the first chakra filling up and spilling over into the sensuous second chakra, filling your pelvis with feeling, with charge, allowing it to move with this excitement, taking more up through your roots to spill over into chakra three, empowering you, strengthening you. Feel it rising up and filling your heart to overflowing, pouring down your arms into your hands. Feel your hands begin to rise with the energy from the earth, to reach out as branches, letting the energy move into your throat chakra, where you can let it out as a sound, welling up from deep below.

Allow the sound to move up into your head, pouring into your third eye and then rising up out of your crown chakra as a trunk reaching for the sky. Reach out with your arms above your head, reach out with your mind into the infinite space above you, calling it down into your trunk, down through your upper chakras, down into your heart, where the celestial energies combine with your earthen energy, making your trunk strong and powerful, energized and cleansed.

Note: When you are done, you may want to touch the ground with your hands to bring all that energy around full circle, back to the earth. This is especially true if you feel spacey or overly charged after doing this exercise. You can use variations on this meditation by adding the colors of the chakras, using their sounds, touching them with your hands, or incorporating movement. Be creative and listen to your body.

Group Ritual

Materials Needed

Rock or other earth object
Inflatable globe
Food to share
Drum or drumming tape

Bodywalk

Establish the boundaries of your sacred space by exploring the room with your body. Begin wherever you are by bringing your awareness to your body and its connection with the ground, feeling the places where you are in actual contact. Move your way around the room, marking the perimeter by experiencing the physical edges with your body, not just your hands. Use parts of you that you wouldn't normally think of—your back, your cheek, your thighs, the back of your upper arm, your shoulder—to connect with the furniture, the walls, the windows, etc.

Calling the Directions

Call out to geographical places you know of in each direction.

Sinking to Earth

While one person drums, slowly drop your body down into the floor, melting, sinking, rolling on the ground, pulling away and then dropping again, deepening your trance as your body sinks and rolls. Finally, the drumming and movement slow down and come to stillness. Remain in that stillness, aware of your body on the floor, breathing, quiet, and alive.

Body Blessing

Use your hands to touch your body, blessing the different parts of you for the functions they serve (i.e. bless my feet for taking me from place to place), the symbolic connections they hold for you (bless my heart for the love and compassion I am able to give and receive), or the aesthetics or pleasurable sensations they bring (bless my genitals for the ecstasy they can give me).

The Earth is Our Mother

Hey Yanna Ho Yanna Hey Yan Yan Yan, The earth is our
Her sacred ground we

moth - er we must take care of her, the earth is our moth - er
walk up - on with ev - ry step we take, her sa-cred ground we walk up - on

we must take care of her.
with ev - ry step we take.

(to beginning)

Charging Earth Object with Prosperity

Take your rock or other object in your hand and feel its weight.
Imagine the place where it came from, its natural habitat. Experience it as a portable piece of the earth, a connection between the moving flesh of your body and the solid, strong body of the earth.

One at a time, participants bring their objects to the altar. Each makes a prosperity wish and binds it into the rock by visualizing the wish entering the rock, becoming one with this solid piece of earth. As an example of how earth can provide, share food, passing it around the circle.

Earth blessing

Pass around an inflatable globe that is currently deflated. Each participant breathes their wishes for the earth's healing into the globe, inflating it as it completes the circle.

Chant

"The Earth is Our Mother..." (see at left).

Grounding

Stand together in a circle, holding hands, and stretch your arms up, breathing in deeply all the energy you've worked with. As you breathe out, let your bodies fold down to the floor and release whatever energy you don't need into the earth. Open the circle, perhaps with a statement that "It is done," or "We have finished," or "Until the next time we meet," or whatever feels appropriate to provide a sense of resolution to the work that you've done.

Resources

Books

Bradshaw, John. *Homecoming*. Bantam.

David, Marc. *Nourishing Wisdom: A New Understanding of Eating*. Bell Tower.

Devall, Bill & Sessions, George. *Deep Ecology*. Peregrine Smith.

Diagram Group. *Man's Body: An Owner's Manual*. Bantam.

Diagram Group. *Woman's Body: An Owner's Manual*. Bantam.

Downer, Carol. *A New View of a Woman's Body*. Feminist Health Press.

Kano, Susan. *Making Peace With Food*. Harper & Row.

Kapit, Wynn & Elson, Lawrence. *The Anatomy Coloring Book*. Harper & Row.

Keleman, Stanley. *The Human Ground*. Center Press.

LaChapelle, Dolores. *Earth Wisdom*. Guild of Tutors Press.

Lehrman, Fredric. *The Sacred Landscape*. Celestial Arts.

Meyers, Dr. Norman. *Gaia: An Atlas of Planet Management*. Anchor Books.

Roberts, Elizabeth & Amidon, Elias, Eds. *Earth Prayers*. Harper.

Music

Danna & Clement. *Gradual Awakening* (A Gradual Awakening)

Eno, Brian. *On Land*

Hamel, Peter Michael. *Nada* (side 1)

Ojas. *Lotusongs II* (side 1, beginning music)
    Trance Tape I (especially side 1)
    Trance Tape II (especially side 2)

Rich, Robert. *Trances* (Hayagriva)

Chakra Two
Water

Getting Started

Assessment

Take time to reflect on the following concepts. Write down whatever thoughts or phrases come to mind about how these concepts operate in your life.

Change   *Sexuality*
Movement   *Sensuality*
Polarity   *Intimacy*
Desire   *Socializing*
Emotions   *Water*
Pleasure

This chakra involves the sacrum, genitals, hips and lower back. How do you feel about these areas of your body? Are there any difficulties you've had in these areas at any time during your life?

Altar Arrangement

Arange your altar to reflect things of the water—shells, cups or a chalice, or a special bowl that could hold water and flowers. Your altar should reflect your feelings, and give you a special sense of pleasure. Sexuality depicted in sculpture or wall art would be a nice addition.

The color for this chakra is orange, which may be difficult to associate with water. You may wish to have an orange candle to remind you of the energetic state, and a cloth on the surface that feels more like the sea.

If you want to work with deities, you may wish to have a picture of the Goddess or God that you find particularly sensual. The ancient god, Pan, is a wonderful second chakra image, as are goddesses or gods of the sea, such as Yemaya, Mari, or Aphrodite.

As always, look over the table of correspondences and the list of concepts and see how you can symbolize the areas that have particular significance for your life.

Correspondences

Sanskrit name	Svadhisthana
Meaning	Sweetness
Location	Sacrum, genitals, affecting hips, knees, lower back
Element	Water
Main Issue	Sexuality, emotions
Goals	Fluidity of movement, pleasure, connection
Malfunction	Stiffness, sexual addiction or sexual anorexia, isolation, emotional instability or numbness
Color	Orange
Planet	Moon
Foods	Liquids
Right	To Feel
Stones	Coral, carnelian
Animals	Fish, alligator
Operating principle	Attraction of opposites
Yoga Path	Tantra
Archetype	Eros

Sharing the Experience

"I'm Sharon and I went through the first chakra with a fine tooth comb. Then I got to the second chakra and I started doing the exercises, and swaying and moving and I said, "Forget it!" I did experience masturbating, and that was something new for me, because I never had permission to do that. I also experienced reaching out more in relationships—in non-sexual relationships—and discovered that friends are actually there for me. So what I really did was share a lot of my feelings this month. And I got a lot of support and a lot of hugs, and that was very healing for me."

•

"I took some time off work to do some first chakra stuff, and I ended up not doing any of it but calling up friends and reaching out and spending a lot of time socializing, actually developing a social life which is something I haven't had outside of my job. I even had a few dates, so that was exciting. I also had the privilege of being present at a birth, and I found it a really amazing experience. I have never particularly wanted children or done child care, but I found it made me look again at all those issues."

•

"For me, this month has been one of experiencing the most powerful emotions. Sadness and tears, anger, where I feel like pulling doors off their hinges, and things I haven't felt in a long time. I've been married 25 years and it seems like we're going through a crisis, and I keep going back and forth about how I feel about it— even hour to hour. I'm learning to flow and learning not to draw conclusions. I've had wonderful second chakra intimacy and bonding with friends as I've gone through this."

•

"I thought the first chakra was easy and I thought I would just breeze through this. But during the second chakra I started feeling sick to my stomach. I've been married 15 years, which seems like forever. I put a lot of weight on in the last few years and I realized it was designed to keep people away. So I'm beginning to make boundaries. I realize sex has not been our issue as much as intimacy. I'm trying to figure out how to get more intimacy between us that isn't necessarily sexual."

•

"I spent every day this month in the Yucatan lying on the beach and looking at the water. So I watched the water and studied it, asking how I could make my life more like water. The waves build up, come in, and break on the sand, move the sand and coral and shells, and then flow back into the ocean, blending together—like I don't do. Sometimes I build up to a wave and don't let it out, but keep it inside. So I want to let things go, recognize it, let it out, and let it flow about me."

Understanding the Concept

Now that we have established our ground and our center, we begin moving upward. As soon as we move, we shift our focus, and discover that the mere act of making a change is a stimulus for consciousness. Change helps us to wake up, to realize there is more to learn, and invites us to reach out and explore. As our attention shifts from *self* (the focus of the first chakra) to *other*, we encounter dualities and their mutual attraction, and discover the realm of feelings and desire. So the first significant aspect of the second chakra is change.

Movement

While the first chakra taught us to be grounded and still, the second chakra allows movement through the body—the movement that begins the journey upward to the crown chakra. Here we work with moving our physical bodies, in addition to learning about the internal movement of emotional energy. Moving our bodies physically promotes flexibility and health. It helps our muscles to relax, and moves chronically blocked energy through the body. It generates the raw energy needed in the third chakra, and can also be a source of pleasure, which is an important element of the second chakra.

Water

The element associated with the second chakra is water. We often refer to emotions as being part of a watery realm—they flow like a river, have tides like the sea, give us raindrops of tears. Water is fluid. It has no shape of its own but follows the shape of the earth below it, or the earthen container that holds it. We can think of our physical bodies as the earthen container and the emotions as the fluid essence that flows through the container. Indeed, we are 97% water! It is our structure that gives shape to the water, but it is the water that fills the structure and allows it to flow and change. So, in keeping with the qualities of water, we want to learn to let our energy yield and flow, cleanse and change.

Duality and Polarity

The second chakra brings us from singleness to *duality*. With duality comes an expansion of the picture, and the presentation of choice. Suddenly there is me and you, this and that, us and them. We make our choices by sorting out our feelings and desires. This work is a prerequisite to enacting the *will*, the work of chakra three.

Duality also brings us the concept of *polarity*, of yin and yang, male and female, up and down, dark and light. We have taken our singleness of chakra one and made a primary division. We now have a line of force running through the middle, connecting the polarities. The ruling force of the second chakra is *attraction of opposites*. This attraction is the basis for movement—an instinctual pull to expand ourselves by experiencing something or someone different from ourselves—the "other." Emotionally we feel this pull as *desire*—a desire to experience something different, a desire to merge with another, a desire to move ourselves to another state of consciousness, a desire to grow.

Emotions

Emotions, from "e" meaning out and "movere" to move, is the moving out of energy in the body, or as John Bradshaw says, "energy in motion." Energy in motion creates expansion and change. Moving upward in the Chakra System is an act of expansion from the condensed state of solid matter to the vastness of consciousness. When we feel a pull towards other, when we feel the tug of desire, of yearning, or emotion, then we are "moved" to initiate something, to make a change, to expand ourselves in some way. If we have a firm foundation as a result of our first chakra work then our ground will be strong enough to allow us to expand without losing our center.

Emotions are the result of *consciousness meeting the body*. If I give you a piece of information, such as saying that you just won the sweepstakes, that information creates an emotional reaction in the body. If I tell you something negative, you might feel sad as a result. Bits of awareness are constantly filtering through the body, creating subtle emotional reactions. Emotions, in turn, are our most physical aspect of awareness. We experience them through sensation. We may often "feel" something before we "know" it consciously. Emotions are the body's gateway to consciousness.

The Pleasure Principle

Complex as they are, emotions can be seen largely as a reaction to pleasure and pain. We experience pleasant emotions over something that *feels* good, that goes the way we want, that affirms us in some way. The less pleasant emotions, such as fear or sadness, result from an experience or expectation of pain. They are the energy in motion needed to make a change to avoid that pain, just as emotions of enthusiasm and joy move us towards pleasure.

Pleasure and pain are outgrowths of the survival mechanism. When survival needs are properly taken care of, the organism naturally turns toward pleasure. Pain is an indication that something is wrong, that something is threatening our survival. If I hit you, or subject you to pain in any way, you will want to pull away from me. When we experience pain, we try to shut down the sensation, and subsequently our feelings. Pain makes us contract, withdraw, and pull our energy inward.

Pleasure, however, encourages us to expand. If we are having our shoulders rubbed, or are being treated to things we enjoy, we tend to relax and allow ourselves to energetically flow and expand. Energy and consciousness are intricately interrelated. If we suppress our feelings, our sensation, and our energetic flow, then we also restrict our consciousness. We limit the amount of change we can experience, and instead our efforts go into keeping things the same. Pleasure then, helps us to expand our consciousness.

Sexuality

Pleasure, emotion, duality and sensation all lead us to sexuality— the expression of opposites merging as one. Sexuality is the experience of attraction, movement, feeling, desire, and connection, all rolled into a joyous experience of pleasure. The sweetness of pleasure is the jewel in the lotus of the second chakra. The Sanskrit name for this chakra, *Svadhisthana*, which means "sweetness," emphasizes this concept.

Second chakra practice involves working on the emotions and sexuality, and on the fluidity of movement through the body.

These are not separate and distinct aspects, but intricately inter-woven. Moving the body can bring up buried emotions or sexual desire. Freeing emotions can help the body move more easily and can allow us to be more open to pleasure. Experiencing pleasure can put us in touch with our bodies and help counteract painful emotions. Each practice can enhance the other aspects.

Blockages

Blocked emotions repress movement and restrict the flow of energy through the second chakra and through the body as a whole. Emotional work is the process of recovering lost feelings, bringing them to life again, experiencing them and resolving them. Unfortunately, emotional work is not always pleasurable. If a feeling was repressed at one time, it may have been painful, and re-experiencing it is a painful process. We feel vulnerable again, sad, angry, or afraid. Once we express and release the emotion, the body's energy is no longer fixated or contracted around that pain, and can expand again into a state of pleasure. Ease and further growth are the result of clearing the body of blocked emotions. The removal of pain increases the capacity for pleasure.

Getting in touch with buried emotions often requires the help of an experienced therapist, or at the very least a trusted friend. We are by nature blind to our own repressed material. Getting the feedback that we seem angry or depressed can help us make deeper contact. It is important when expressing feelings, especially difficult ones, that we have a listener who is non-judg-mental, who does not argue about our "right" to be angry or sad, but who is willing to merely witness and sympathize. Reclaiming the *right to feel* is one of the tasks of the second chakra, and we need a helper who can assist with this.

The goal of healing the second chakra is to have a healthy flow of emotional energy through the body, to be able to fully experience pleasure through movement and sexuality, and to be able to experience change and enhancement as a result of connect-ing with concepts, people, and events that are different from our own baseline of reality.

Excess and Deficiency

If the second chakra is energetically deficient, there is fear of change. Energy gets trapped in the structural aspects of the first chakra, and resists fluidity, becoming hard like earth. We may seem "flat" or dull emotionally, or we may have difficulty feeling emotions at all. There may be a tendency to avoid pleasure and a distinct lack of sensuality in appearance and behavior. We may scoff at pleasure as a distraction from "true work." We may fear or reject it out of a sense of shame. There may be little passion, and an overly developed sense of self-control.

If the chakra is excessive or too open, the opposite applies. We may be overly emotional, constantly swinging back and forth between extremes, ruled by emotions, rather than allowing them to flow through. We may be overly influenced by other people's emotions, suffering from a lack of boundaries. There may be sexual addiction, or a constant need for pleasurable stimulation, entertainment, partying, and social interaction. An excessive second chakra scatters the liberating energy too soon, so it does not flow through to the higher chakras.

Ideally, we should be able to embrace polarities, feel our emotions, and express ourselves sexually without losing the connection with our own center. The center of polarity is a state of balance. We must be willing to embrace both sides to achieve balance. The joining together of polarities forms the metaphorical basis for power, the goal of the next step of our climb, chakra three.

Working with Movement

In our culture, moving the pelvis is often considered lewd or at least provocative. Many students find the movements of the second chakra embarrassing, and in classes there is laughter and blushing as students push through their inhibitions. One older student commented that he had never moved his hips in this manner before, and that the movements reminded him of burlesque.

It's not surprising that opening the sexual chakra physically brings up so many of our feelings about sexuality. The overt sexuality and sensuality of the second chakra movements may not be appropriate in many situations that you find yourself in daily life. It would certainly disrupt business meetings if you began to swing your pelvis from side to side as you presented a proposal. On the other hand, rigidly holding the pelvic area immobile blocks the energy flow through your entire system. That same presentation might seem dry and "juiceless" if you are holding back the natural sensual flow of your energy through the body. Finding the balance begins with removing the inhibitions that keep the movement in check. You may find this easier in private, without an audience to trigger discomfort from flaunting the unspoken rules of "appropriate" behavior.

Goddess Pose

We begin with a quiet pose designed to open the groin and allow you to experience a state of vulnerability and receptivity. Lying on your back, bend your knees and pull your feet up towards your buttocks along the floor. Let your knees open out to the sides, allowing the weight of your legs to stretch open the insides of your thighs. Don't worry about how far down your knees open, just allow yourself to experience the open feeling. The two photos show two possibilities for how wide your knees might open—let gravity open you to wherever your flexibility allows, without forcing.

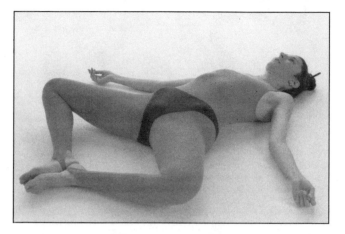

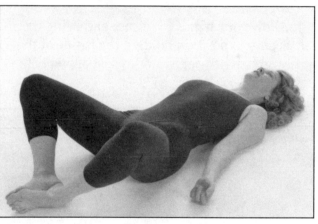

Pelvic Rocks

From the goddess pose, bring your knees together and pull them up towards your chest, grabbing onto one wrist with the other hand and allowing the weight of your arms to passively press your legs inwards. Bring your attention to your sacrum and lower back, and experiment with gently pressing the lower back down towards the floor and then shifting to press the sacrum down. This subtle rocking movement will shift the area of physical stimulation and stretch, opening up the second chakra area.

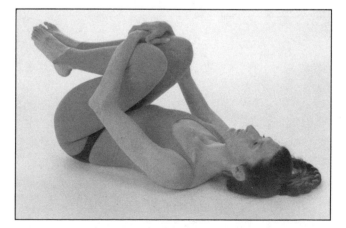

Pelvic Side Rolls

1 Allow your hands to release and bring them each to a position holding the inside of the knee. Stretch here for as long as feels appropriate.

2 Bring your right arm out to the side along the ground. The left knee falls slowly over to the left to touch the ground.

3 The right leg remains open as long as it can and then folds down on top of the left leg. Straighten your left arm out to the side and move to the other side by lifting the top leg (the right in this case) slowly off the bottom leg and opening it, allowing the left leg to continue to fall open to the left, until the right leg comes all the way down to the ground on the right and the left leg folds down on top of it. Perform this movement loosely, allowing gravity to do most of the work and using only the muscles necessary to create the movement. Bring your attention to the pelvic area and the genitals as you move.

Pelvic Side Rolls continue the theme of the Goddess Pose, opening the groin, but here the emphasis is on the flow of opening and closing as you move easily from side (closed) through center (open) to side and back again.

Pelvic Side Rolls with Straight Legs

1 As you finish the right side and bring the right leg over onto the left, straighten both legs.

2 Lift the right leg into the air and circle it up and over to the right, much the same as with the legs bent in the previous movement, but keep the legs strongly contracted (knees straight). Bring the right leg down to the floor to the right of your body and let the left leg release onto the right.

This variation of Pelvic Side Rolls adds the contrast of passive opening at the groin with the active contraction of the muscles of the leg to maintain straight knees. This tension/relaxation dichotomy is characteristic of the second chakra. It is a familiar attribute of sexuality, where we find both tension and relaxation essential to our ability to participate fully in the body's excitation and release.

Child's Pose—Open Hips

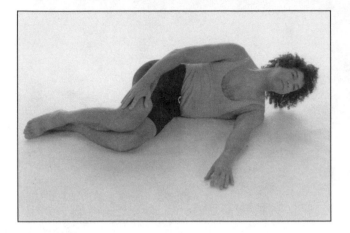

1 End your side to side roll on one side (I'll use the left side for illustration) and swing the right arm around to your right leg, so you are lying on your left side and facing to the left.

2 Bring your right hand over to the ground near your knees.

3 Begin to push against the floor with both arms as you shift your weight over until you are sitting on your legs with your torso still folded forward. Allow your knees to move apart.

Child's Pose—Open Hips (continued)

4 Shift the torso from side to side by moving the hip joints loosely. Lift your torso enough to allow the movement emanating from your pelvis to travel up your spine, instigating the movement from the second chakra. Once the movement is flowing, allow it to travel through you and out your head and arms, spiraling your attention back to the pelvis again, as it continues to generate movement and carry energy up from the root chakra, through the dancing second chakra, and onwards into the rest of your body.

Downward Faced Puppy

Bring your legs closer to each other, in line with your thigh sockets, and stretch your torso forward. This pose can open the upper chest and heart chakra, but for now focus on the opening that happens in the groin area when you tilt the top of the pelvis forward (as if reaching the front of the hip bones towards the thighs).

Cat

1 Bring your weight onto your hands and knees and stop for a moment to feel the length of your spine. Be aware of its natural curves.

2 On an outbreath, begin to roll your spine up towards the ceiling, allowing your head to hang forward, neck released.

3 As you breathe in again roll your spine into an arch, tilting the pelvis forward and lifting your neck and head while your shoulders pull down and back and away from your ears. Continue this arch and release cycle for as many breaths as you like.

4 Then sway your hips side to side, allowing your torso to arch sideways, leaning your head towards the same direction as your tail. Eventually, let the movement become more spontaneous, exploring a dance that originates in your pelvis and moves throughout your body, the only restriction being to keep your hands and feet on the floor.

Open Legs

This

Not this

1 Find a flowing way to move from hands and knees to sitting on your buttocks with your legs in front of you. Open your feet as far as is comfortable, keeping your knees loose. Imagine your spine lifting away from the floor, starting at the bottom and working your way up your back, shoulders dropping away from ears, long neck, feeling the lengthening move up through the top of your head and out. Be careful not to round your back.

Open Legs (continued)

2 You can keep your hands on the ground behind you if this helps you to align your spine. You might try this with your knees straight, but if that rounds your lower back, practice with knees bent until you are more flexible.

3 Bring your arms in front of you and begin to tilt your pelvis forward, pulling it through your legs by rotating in your hip socket as you imagine your spine continuing to lengthen.

This exercise, in addition to opening the groin, brings attention to the relationship of the pelvis to the legs and to the rest of the spine. Loosening up the hip joints provides more freedom of movement for the pelvis.

Transition through Squat

Bring your legs together in front of you, resting lightly on your hands on the floor behind you. Push against the floor with your hands and shift your weight into the squat. Roll up to standing in the same way as in the first chakra (see pg. 55).

Standing Hip Practice

This section of movements of the pelvis are the basis for the second chakra dance. As you begin to practice them, focus on isolating the pelvis, keeping the head and upper body and the feet in place. The movements originate in the second chakra, and though they eventually radiate out from there through the rest of the body, the first step is to practice containing the movements in the pelvis area, and to gain control over the direction and thrust of the movements. This does not mean rigidly holding the head and shoulders in place, but rather keeping them relaxed and uninvolved at first.

Forward and Back Tilts

1 With knees slightly bent, tighten the buttocks and press the pubis forward, flattening the natural curve in the lower back.

2 Allow the lower back to slowly arch as you tilt the top of your pelvis forward, folding slightly at the thigh socket.

 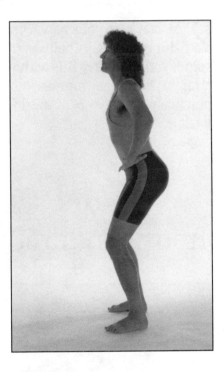

Standing Hip Practice (continued)

Side shifts

Find the place where your pelvis feels balanced on its forward-back axis. Move your pelvis gently from side to side, keeping your body quiet above the waist. Center the movement in the thigh socket and abdomen. Allow the legs and knees to do what they need to support your movement.

Circling

Create circles with your hips by combining the previous two movement patterns. Be sure to practice circling in both directions.

Free movement

Now let yourself go, creating patterns and figures in the air with your hips as they circle, shift, sway, and dance through all the possible movements available to them. Your arms flow along with your movements, but don't shift the focus to them. Let them express a movement flow that originates in your second chakra, rather than moving on their own.

Water Walking

Continue the movement of the standing hip practice, but allow your feet to leave the floor now as you move, stepping to the side, front, back, wherever your pelvis movement takes you. Visualize yourself walking through water or imagine that your body is water, flowing like a river, rolling like ocean waves.

The Dance

If you've followed the sequence to water walking, you are already doing the second chakra dance, gliding and flowing through the space available to you. Your dance may take you back down to the floor, sensuously pushing and pulling and rolling, or you may use your hands to stabilize you on the floor, wall, or piece of furniture, allowing your hips freedom to move. The initiation of each flow of movement comes from your pelvis, but the sensuality travels through each cell of your body, each ripple of muscle and flesh, each shift of weight.

Your dance of water may take on the energy flows of the ocean: great waves, pounding surf, tides moving in and out. The quiet reflection of a lake or pond yields an entirely different movement quality, with gentle ripples flowing from one part of your body to another. Perhaps your dance will reflect the excitement and force of the rapids, rushing and crashing and wild.

Just as sexual interactions can vary from sweet, silly, or humorous to passionate, aggressive, quietly intense, or timelessly transcendent, your dance can cover a range of sensual expressions through movement. Let your body lead you without the censorship of your mind and social programming. Dancing alone at first may be extremely important in this regard—fear of the judgments of others can be a powerful constrictor of movement. Later, when you've developed some confidence and comfort in your dancing and some trust in those you want to share it with, you may find it easier to dance your dance with others.

Bioenergetic Movement: Connecting the Pelvis

This exercise begins with the basic bioenergetic grounding described in chakra one (page 59). If you have been practicing it for awhile already, you are now familiar with the sensation of allowing the charge of energy from the earth to flow through your legs and into your first chakra. If not, continue with the first chakra a bit longer before adding this section. If the energy doesn't yet flow through your legs, it's not likely to flow into your second chakra, as the legs are part of the channel we are working with.

Quickly reviewing, you will remember that you are standing firmly on both feet, planted about shoulder width apart. Your knees are bent, and you are building up a charge of energy in your legs by inhaling and bending your knees, and exhaling and pushing your feet into the earth as your knees straighten. Remember, in this exercise you do not straighten your knees all the way.

When you feel that your legs have made the connection you can add the following to what you are already doing:

1 As you bend your knees and inhale, pull your buttocks back by allowing your pelvis to tip backward, as if swinging on a pin through your waistline. Keep your back in place—all this movement is through the pelvis. Let your hands do whatever feels right.

2 As you exhale and push your feet into the ground, also push your pelvis for-ward. When you inhale, once again bend your knees, pull your pelvis backward, and re-peat the sequence, again and again.

Connecting the Pelvis (continued)

The object of this exercise is to move the energy that is coursing through your legs up past the first chakra and into the second chakra. You may find stiffness that needs working through, or you may find the movement quite easy. As you focus on the pelvis, don't forget that you are still getting the energy from the floor, through your feet and legs. Don't lose your ground while you focus on something new!

Continue the movement until you feel something happen inside—some change in your lower body. You may feel sexual energy start to fill your pelvis, or you may feel a flow of emotional energy. You may get shaking or trembling—which is a sign that the energy is flowing into a new place. Relax and let it flow and shake.

The second chakra is about change and movement, and this exercise allows our bodies to change and move.

When you have done it long enough for your purposes, come to a stop at a place that feels like it has the most energy. (This is where the knees are bent somewhat and the pelvis is tipped into whatever angle produces the most sensation.) See if you can still feel the energy streaming. Slowly come to a centered standstill and take time to feel your body. Walk around the room and see if you can feel any effects.

It may take a lot of practice to feel this exercise deeply. Be patient with yourself and try to enjoy the process.

Partner Work: Stretching and Balancing

1 Stand facing your partner and take hands, wrapping your hands around your partner's to hold at the wrist and vice versa.

2 Slowly back away from each other, bending at the hip joint rather than the mid-back. Each of you keeps your feet hip width apart with your feet parallel. Back away until you are both allowing your weight to fall away from each other, depending on the balance between you to keep you from falling. Keep your arms straight so that you are not attempting to hold yourself up with your arm muscles. Unless you have lower back problems, straighten your knees and allow the weight of your partner pulling you to stretch out your hamstrings at the backs of your thighs. Adjust the position of your feet to maintain the balance between you as you both settle into the stretch. Think about lifting your sitting bones up towards the ceiling and dropping your pelvis forward towards your thighs. To come up, bend your knees and walk slowly towards each other as you raise your torsos.

This exercise has several functions related to the second chakra. As you lift the sitting bones up, the genital area opens, directly affecting the second chakra sexuality. In addition, there is the connection and trust that occurs with your partner when you are able to surrender to the balance between you.

3 Now take only one of your partner's hands, either the same hand or the opposite hand, again holding at the wrists for stability. Allow your weight to fall away from each other, this time maintaining an upright posture. Play with the balance, reaching away with your free arm, circling it in the air, experimenting with lifting one of your legs, etc.

Partner Work: Back to Back Connection

1 Stand back to back with your partner with your knees bent slightly and release your weight into your partner's back. You are standing on your own two feet, but your balance point is between the two of you. If your partner was not there you would fall backwards. Notice the sensations in your back and the pressure of this other body against you. Which parts of your back are making the connection? If you find that only your upper back is touching your partner's, see if you can allow your lower backs to connect as well. Be aware of your breathing, and see if you can sense your partner's breathing, both of you expanding into each other with each inhalation, relaxing into each other with each exhalation.

2 Begin slowly to move against each other, imagining that you are having a conversation with your backs. Be sensitive to your partner's movement and find ways to flow into movement together. When you have danced together for a while, allow your arms to join the dance. When it feels done, find an appropriate way to end your dance rather than stopping abruptly. Honor the energy that you have shared together.

Group Work: Dance

Each participant dances their own second chakra dance (see page 102) around the space you are working in, becoming aware of the dances of the other participants. As you feel drawn, join with another dancer, dancing with them, touching or not as you both desire, exploring your connection with this other person. You might join both hands as you dance together, or just join one and let the other arm dance free. You might connect back to back and see where that connection leads you together. You could spontaneously take turns leading movements while the other imitates the leader's movements, or one of you might lead the other by the hand, skipping and jumping and dancing around the room. When you feel ready, find a way to say farewell with your movements, and dance on to another person or do your own dance for awhile (this is especially important if you tend to accommodate your partner to the point of losing touch with your own dance).

Long, flowing scarves can be an enjoyable addition to this group dance, inspiring a flowing grace in individual, partner and group movements. Dancing with scarves allows you to connect with each other through the medium of holding and playing with the scarf together without actually touching bodies. You may join in groups larger than two, forming clumps of dancers, and then moving on or joining with others. Let the music bring your dance to a close, or find a natural ending point for the dance spontaneously.

Putting It Into Practice

Listed below are topics related to the second chakra and suggestions for how to work with them. Take your time, savoring the teaching that each one brings. Since this chakra is about pleasure, enjoy the process!

Sex

Sexuality is the expression of second chakra energy. It follows logically from desire, emotion, and pleasure. It is an ultimate experience of union with another—the dance of duality and the movement of energy through the body, the ecstasy of pleasure.

If you are in a sexual relationship, be creative and explore. Try something new, talk about your feelings about sex, buy some sexy underwear, see an erotic movie, or read an erotic book, or work with an erotic self-help books with your partner.

If you are not in a relationship, create a fantasy of who you would like your next partner to be—what kind of sexual relationship you would like to have, how you would like it to feel, how it would nourish you. Make love to yourself, involving your whole body in the process. You can also do a lot of the things listed above, such as buying underwear, seeing an erotic movie, or just talking about sex to friends you trust.

Alone, or with someone you trust, allow yourself to move sensuously, to pay attention to the feeling of textures, smells, tastes. Sensations of all sorts are part of our feelings, our stimulation to consciousness, and our pleasure. Attune yourself to sensations everywhere and notice how they affect you.

Movement

Just as chakra one was about getting settled and learning to be still and contain, chakra two is about movement and reaching out. It is about attuning to the movement that arises from within. Movement helps to put us in our body, and helps the energy flow through us in a continuous, nourishing fashion.

Notice your movements throughout the day as you do your daily activities. Whenever you think of it, stretch, wiggle, adjust, make yourself more comfortable.

Allow yourself the pleasure of movement at least once a day. Put on some music and dance in your living room, paying attention to your body's need for expression rather than following any set form. Find tight places in your body and see what kind of movements help to release them. Try moving that energy through to other parts of your body. Experiment with movement as part of your personal expression. What movements are really you? What movements express your feelings? What movements awaken your feelings?

Make time for the movements described in the movement section, as it is so vitally important to this chakra.

Change

The real essence of the second chakra is change. When we travel from one to two, from stability to movement, from survival to pleasure, we experience change. Avoiding change blocks the second chakra. If you've learned to properly ground yourself through the first chakra work, you should not need to cling to the security of staying with the same old things now.

Think of something different to do. If you always drive to work along the same route, purposely pick another route. If you always wear dark colors, wear light colors. If you are talkative, be quiet; if you are quiet, push yourself to interact more. Watch out for statements like "I never do that—it's just not me," as a clue to a pattern that you could change. Notice the effect it has on your consciousness and your sense of aliveness when you do something completely out of character for yourself.

Water

Water is the element of chakra two. Spend time in or around water—go swimming, visit a river, a lake, or the ocean. Indulge in the pleasures of water in the form of hot baths, hot tubs, or long showers. Study the essence of water, how it moves, how it flows. Pay special attention to your water rituals like bathing or taking a shower, making coffee or watering your plants. Pay attention to your need for liquid and how it feels as it goes into your body.

Nurturing

When we add up all the attributes of the second chakra: water, sex, pleasure, emotion, movement, change—they all describe ways of nurturing and nourishing. So above all NURTURE YOURSELF! Do what feels right. Be good to yourself.

Journal Exercises

1. Desire

Desire is the fruit of the body (chakra 1) and the fuel of the will (chakra 3). Desire is that which gets us up off our butts (chakra 1), reaching out and expanding to encompass more than just ourselves. Now that we have consolidated what we have, it is time to look at what we want.

Take time to get in touch with your desires. Make a list of them. Notice how many of them are desires of the body, desires of the mind, spirit, ego, or whatever. Wanting to sleep more, for example, is a desire of the body. Wanting to read a book might be a desire of the mind. Wanting a Ph.D. could be a desire of the mind, or perhaps of the ego.

Next, notice if any of your desires are mutually exclusive. You may desire more money while simultaneously desiring more time off work. Which is more important? (In the third chakra we will evolve our desires into goals, as we address the will.)

2. Emotions

Emotions are closely related to desires. Anger arises out of a desire to be treated better, sadness out of the loss of something we desired, happiness from a desire granted. Focus on your emotions—examine how they rule your life, examine what you do with them, how they affect your energy, and take note of which emotions affect you most strongly.

At the end of each day, take a moment to review the emotions you have passed through. Draw a little calendar in your journal and jot down some notes that chart your emotional travels. You might even draw a face that reflects your mood each day so that at the end of the month you can look at your faces and get an overall emotional picture of yourself.

Emotion is the motion of energy out of the body. When we block an emotion, we block the energy flow through the chakras. Allow yourself to let go of the places you are blocking. This doesn't mean venting your anger or tears on anyone that happens by whenever you feel like it, but rather creating a time and place where you can let your waters flow. It also means letting go of old angers and pains that inhibit you but are no longer serving a positive purpose. This is the time to clear those old feelings out so that they don't get in the way later. Writing them down can be instrumental in this process.

3. Pleasure

Desire and emotions have a lot to do with pleasure and pain. Pleasure is an impetus to move toward; pain makes us move away. This is the time to pleasure yourself!

Make a list of the things that give you pleasure. (How does it compare to your list of desires?) Again, try to see that there are pleasures listed for all parts of you—your body, your mind, your spirit, your emotions, your creativity, etc. Work on creating some bit of pleasure for yourself every day, and aim for overall balance in a week to nourish all parts of you. Notice how you feel about yourself and how the amount of pleasure in your life affects your self esteem.

How much do you do for yourself daily that is for your own pleasure? How much guilt do you have to deal with when you allow yourself pleasure? How does pleasure make you feel? What priority does it have in your life? Are you happy with that?

4. Duality

One of the prime forces for movement in the universe is the attraction of opposites, a force that comes about by virtue of the existence of duality. This is the time to pay attention to opposites.

• What qualities are opposite to your own and how do you feel about them?

• What do you repress in yourself? How are you polarized?

• One polarity we dance between is the male/female duality. How much do you ac-knowledge your female side? Your male side?

Take time to acknowledge your shadow. The shadow is the part of the personality that we reject as being unpleasant, unethical, or undesirable. Our shadow might be the part of us that is angry, selfish, lazy, or sloppy. Acknowledgment of the shadow does not mean that we emphasize these qualities, but that we acknowledge their existence directly, so that they do not infiltrate our actions. If my shadow is an angry bitch, I might want to acknowledge it by looking at where the anger comes from, and what function it would have in my life.

• What form would your shadow take if you were to allow its expression?

• What kind of feelings would be operating?

• How are those feelings affecting your life presently?

Emotions are the energetic expression of the second chakra. Many of us experience dualities in our emotional fluctuations: we range from happy to sad, from hopeful to discouraged, from angry to placating. Ideally, we want a full range of emotions, so that we can encompass both polarities, yet be centered and balanced within their range. If we are only able to experience one side, then we are emotionally unbalanced. If we are so caught in the fluctuations that we cannot feel the middle ground, we can lose our sense of self, and become victims of our own emotional flow.

• How much do your emotions vary between one extreme and the other?

• What are the most common poles?

• Do they balance over time?

• What would be a middle ground expression of these emotions?

Ideally, the Inner Self is the meeting point of all dualities. In this chakra we work to let go of polarization and come to a balance, without denial or repression. Instead we look for the integration that allows us to progress upward through the chakras from a firm and solid ground with an enlivening charge of emotional energy.

5. Reassessment

• What have you learned about yourself as you've worked through the activities for the second chakra?

• What areas of this chakra do you need to work on? How will you do that?

• What areas of this chakra do you feel pleased with? How can you utilize these strengths?

• What changes have you made and how do you feel about them?

Entering Sacred Space

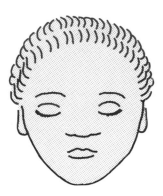

Sea Altar Meditation

A pleasant ritual in honor of the sea can be done by those who live near a body of water that has a tide. Begin at low tide and collect shells, driftwood, seaweed and other objects from the beach. Pick a spot to make a mandala on the beach out of these objects. Make it into a design that makes a statement for you—it could be a peace sign, a yin-yang, a dedication to a sea goddess, or a joint creation with a loved one. When you finish, meditate on the mandala and then watch the tide come in and take it away.

Ritual for Balancing Polarity

Often in our lives, we find ourselves bouncing back and forth between two choices, unable to consolidate two seemingly opposite parts of ourselves. This is part of the dance of polarity, and usually, if a decision between two choices is not apparent, it is because each side has considerable merit and neither choice alone quite answers the problem.

The following ritual is a simple one and can be done alone or with a group of any size. Make room to walk in a circle, as large as your chosen space allows. Mark out in your mind the path of the circle and remove any obstacles along that path.

Sit in meditation long enough to get in touch with the two sides of your equation. It may be something practical like whether to quit your job or stay with it, or whether to move to a new house. It may be the need to resolve different parts of yourself, such as the part that wants to be alone and the part that wants to be social. Or it may be the need to balance a polarity you have been caught in lately, such as work and play, passivity and aggression, activity and quiet. It is important for this exercise to pick only one set of polarities at a time, but you can repeat the ritual as often as you like.

Look at your circle and draw a mental line across the diameter. You may even wish to mark it with a stick or some narrow object. Now allow one side of the circle to be one side of the polarity and the other side to represent its opposite. For instance, if I am trying to sort out my conflict about home and career, I might make the right side of the circle represent career, and the left side represent my home life.

Walk slowly around the circle in one direction. When you are on one side of the circle, immerse yourself in the feeling that side brings up for you. When I walk on the career side, I immerse myself in the feeling I have when I am doing my work, traveling, giving workshops, doing promotion, writing, etc. When I pass the midpoint of the circle and enter into the side that represents home, I immerse myself in the feelings of being at home with my family, relaxing, cooking, being quiet.

Walk around the circle several times. Each time you pass the midpoint, you change to the other polarity, totally immersing yourself in its reality and paying attention to how that feels in your body. Allow your body to express these feelings as you walk. You might walk tall and proud on one side and hunch over on the other, or you might walk fast on one side and slow on the other.

When you have walked around the circle several times, and have felt each side, then you are ready to walk down the middle. As you do so, try to incorporate a balance between the two extremes. Imagine yourself doing both at once, incorporating the energy of the fast and the peacefulness of the slow, the excitement of one side and the restfulness of the other. Notice how it feels in your body. See if you can now walk through the room like this. Notice any feelings of resolution.

Group Ritual

One person can guide the group through all the sections, or different people might take different sections to lead.

Materials Needed

A cup for each participant
Pitcher of water
Live musicians or taped music (suggestions are given but you may chose whatever music seems appropriate)

Creating Sacred Space

Join hands in a circle and then turn around to face the outside of the circle. One participant leads the group in grounding, sinking roots deep into the earth. Continue from there with the following imagery.

As you bring energy up into your body, bring it into your first chakra and imagine it glowing red and spinning. It cleans out the sphere of earth energy, balancing it as it spins, then proceeds up through each chakra in turn. Imagine it glowing the appropriate color and spinning, balancing. When you get to the seventh chakra at the top of the head, visualize the energy that you've brought up through your chakras bursting open at the crown, opening you to connection with universal energy that can then enter through your crown and pour down through your chakras, mixing with the earth energy that came up from the roots in the earth.

Sense the people on both sides of you and allow your hands to reach out enough for the backs of your hands to touch. Visualize the energy circulating through each of you moving out of each hand and into the hands of the people on either side of you, creating a circular energy flow that moves around the circle and back into you again. When this energy circulating around the circle feels strong and stable, bring your arms forward, then reach them slowly up, creating an arc that sweeps up towards the sky, where your upraised arms meet the hands on either side of you. This creates an energy sphere surrounding the entire circle.

Now each participant turns to face the inside of the circle, arms still raised with the energy. Visualize your arms completing the top of the sphere as they come forward to reach towards the center of the group.

Invoking Elements

Using music, the whole group moves freely through the ritual space, allowing their bodies to become each element, facing the appropriate directions. The movement of each element may be different for each participant. For example, one person moving as air may swoop their arms through space in large, energetic movements as they imagine strong winds. Another may tiptoe lightly while their arms and head sway gently.

For fire, the movements may reflect flames leaping and dancing wildly, or they might be small sparks of energy flickering, or perhaps volcanoes erupting. Water movements could be gently flowing like a stream, or the rhythmic in and out of the tides, or perhaps the dance of the rain falling. Earth may inspire large, slow, steady movements, or perhaps you might find yourself rolling on the ground, or beating a heartbeat with your foot on the floor. These are just some of the many possibilities—the dance will emerge from your own unique interpretations of each element.

Music: Air (East) *Dream Theory in Malay.* (These
                    Times) Hassell
            Fire (South) *Drums of Passion.* Olatunji
            Water (West) *Dream Theory in Malay.* (Gift of
                    Fire) Hassell
            Earth (North) *Lotusongs II.* Ojas

Evoke Deity

Each participant becomes the receptive, nurturant body of the Goddess—fertile earth ready to support growth and provide sustenance. Each then becomes the God in the form of the spirit of life springing from within, sprouting and growing into ripeness, maturity.

Music: *Cymbalom Solos.* Michael Masley

Working with Energy

Each participant dances their dance, with the hips and pelvis leading the movements. Join with partners whenever, however and for as long as you will.

Music: *Dancing Toward the One.* Gabrielle Roth & the
                    Mirrors

The Waterfall Song

Words and music by Anodea Judith

Let the wa - a - ter fall, let the wa - ter fall let the wa - ter fall on the

earth.   Let the   trees   grow tall   Let the   wa - ter fall   Let the

green - e - ry grow on the   earth.

Chant & Communion

As the movement slows down and comes to a stop, all melt to the floor to rest in silence. All sing while each participant's cup is filled from a communal pitcher of water.

(See the Waterfall Song above)

Grounding

Participants recreate the circle, arms around each other. Acknowledge and release all that has been evoked. Acknowledge the energy you raised and danced with and send any excess back down into the earth, bringing the circle down with it.

Resources

Books

Abbott, Frankin, ed. *Men & Intimacy*. The Crossing Press.

Anand, Margo. *The Art of Sexual Ecstacy*. Jeremy Tarcher.

Barbach, Lonnie. *For Each Other: Sharing Sexual Intimacy*. Signet.

Bonheim, Jalaja. *The Serpent and the Wave: A Guide to Movement Meditation*. Celestial Arts.

Chia, Mantak & Maneewan. *Healing Love through the Tao: Cultivating female sexual energy*. Healing Tao Books.

Douglas, Nik & Slinger, Penny. *Sexual Secrets*. Destiny.

Hawthorne, Nan. *Loving the Goddess Within: Sex Magick for Women*. Delphi Press.

Ramsdale, David Alan and Ellen Jo. *Sexual Energy Ecstasy*. Peak Skill Publishing,

Williams, Brandy. *Ecstatic Ritual: Practical Sex Magick*. Avery Pub.

Music

Hassell, Jon. *Dream Theory in Malay*.

Masley, Michael. *Cymbalom Solos*.

Khan, Al Gromer. *Divan I Khas*.

Roth, Gabrielle & The Mirrors. *Dancing Toward the One*.

> *Initiation.*
>
> *Ritual.*
>
> *Totem.*
>
> *Waves.*

Roth, Schawkie. *Dance of the Tao*.

Catalogs

Good Vibrations
1210 Valencia Street
San Francisco, Ca 94110

Chakra Three
Fire

Getting Started

Where Are You Now?

The following words are key concepts related to the third chakra. Look at each word and meditate on it for a few moments. Then free associate by writing whatever thoughts or images come to mind. Note that the concepts listed include both positive and negative aspects of the third chakra.

Power	*Authority*
Will	*Aggression*
Energy	*Warrior*
Metabolism	*Transformation*
Ease	*Warmth*
Humor	*Fire*
Control	

This chakra involves the solar plexus, between the navel and the base of the sternum. How do you feel about this area of your body? Are there any difficulties you've had in this area at any time during your life?

Altar Arrangement

Begin by redressing your altar in yellow. Notice the energy and vitality of the bright yellow color, and notice its effect on you. Since our element in this chakra is fire, you may want to feature candles or an oil lamp as representatives of fire. Read the table of correspondences and add anything appropriate to the altar, being conscious of the purpose of every item you place on it. It is important in the third chakra to remain conscious of *purpose* in all actions.

In this chakra we are looking at our will, examining where we are going with our lives and exerting the energy necessary to get there. On your altar you might place objects that are symbolic of your goals and sense of purpose in life. Create a collage of images that reflect your direction and who you want to be in the world and place this on or above your altar.

The ritual we use in the third chakra (see page 151) involves writing our objectives on a candle. After doing the ritual, place your candle in the center of your altar, and light it whenever you are doing your meditations or exercises until it burns to the bottom.

Correspondences

Sanskrit name	Manipura
Meaning	Lustrous gem
Location	Solar plexus, between navel and base of sternum
Element	Fire
Main Issue	Power, energy
Goals	Vitality, strength of will, sense of purpose, effectiveness
Malfunction	*Excessive:* Inability to slow down, need to be in control, rage addiction, stomach ulcers, excessive weight around middle. *Deficient:* Timidity, low energy or chronic fatigue, addiction to stimulating substances, submissive approach to life, digestive troubles
Color	Yellow
Planet	Mars (also related to the sun)
Foods	Complex carbohydrates
Right	To Act
Stones	Topaz, amber
Animals	Ram, lion
Operating principle	Combustion
Yoga Path	Karma yoga
Archetype	Magician, Warrior

Sharing the Experience

"I'm Sally and I've been going through some wild, fiery stuff this month. I've been raging, angry, and antagonized for about a week. I woke up at 7 in the morning and wrote a seventeen-page letter to my mother, who's a rageaholic. This has opened up a lot of other things too, creating openings in my upper chakras. But it's really getting my energy moving in a way that has been previously stuck."

•

"I'm Sue and I had some third chakra things come up. The one day a month when I need to stay away from people and be by myself, I was expected to get three jobs done in one day. It probably could have been done if I had the support of my coworkers, but I didn't get the support. After about two thirds of the day I blew up like a volcano—exploded. Passed it on to everybody. I hate doing that though because then I have to deal with the consequences. I told my boss that if you want me to do this job, you're going to have to give the support I need, and leave me alone the third week of the accounting period. And I think he got it."

•

"I'm John and I've had an interesting month. The universe provided me with third chakra challenges. I am being challenged to hold my ground, to take care of myself. There seems to have been a kind of synergy in this. To deal with

the issues that were threatening myself and my wife, and to hold our relationship clear, and at the same time protect our space, knowing that somebody else was going to take responsibility for something. And then being challenged to do the same thing again with somebody else. Being invaded, violated and being able to say No. Having to tell the policeman whether I want to prosecute. Not wanting to, but being told that there could be no protection unless I was willing. Knowing that might make someone unhappy and doing it anyway because it was right."

•

"My name's Georgia and I'm in love. It's really happening. I am very happy, feel very powerful, not in control, like I usually do, but still really powerful and present and wonderful. I know that may be more of a fourth chakra thing, but I'm noticing how powerful it makes me feel."

•

"I'm Janet and I had maybe three issues when I joined this class. One was my boss taking all of my power. Two was feeling unloved and wanting a partner, and three was not having any money. And in the last thirty days since we met, I've filed a discrimination suit against my boss, and took my power there. Now he's on the defensive, which makes me feel powerful. I got a $200 a month raise. And I fell in love! I feel great!"

"I'm Katherine and this month the internal fire has been incredible. I feel that all I broke loose in the first and second chakra has been channeled here in the third chakra and I've had a glorious month. Everything is working. I've been making money. I channeled a whole course and taught it. It just feels like my power has been so strong that I have just empowered everyone that's been around. I've found it to flow real easily. And when I've had to stand up for myself, it felt like I was able to hold my ground, and it didn't feel like a struggle. I requested a high price for a job I was doing and got that, as well as offers for more. I was challenged several times on it, even down to signing the contract and I held my ground each time. It feels like a shared power. I've felt good about everyone I've worked with all month."

•

"I'm Gabrielle and I did not have a wonderful month. I had a very third chakra month, but it wasn't wonderful. I got in touch with my anger, how I repress it, how I'm supposed to be a nice girl, and I just ran my anger and it was painful for me. I also noticed how I'll sit in my pain instead of moving it, and I found myself using my anger to move it, and I found myself moving it into activity or communication. All month I felt this pressure on my heart, and sometimes a release where it would turn into loving feelings. It was tough though because I am not at all comfortable with anger. Now for the good news! My goal was to get a job doing something I love, and I got a job in 'energy'! I'm going to be an educator to teach people how to conserve energy. And I love it!"

•

"I'm Karlin and I worked on a lot of power issues. I'm a go-between in my job between upper management and middle management, so I got to be diplomatic and deal with power issues and got lots of practice in learning to stay with myself. I made definite decisions to give up parts of myself at about six years old, and I've been working to reclaim it."

•

"I'm Jeanette and I used the third chakra energy to get myself to do things I've been putting off. I did some writing and made a budget, and started walking to work, and dealt with some old relationship issues. I finally sent off a letter I had written asking for information about opportunities. I've accomplished a lot this month, doing things I had put off, and the third chakra came out and lit that spark and got it all done, and it feels really good."

Understanding the Concept

With our bodies grounded and our feelings flowing, we are ready to begin work on developing chakra three, the chakra that relates to *personal power, will,* and *vitality*. This is where we take action, create change, reorganize for efficiency, and purify ourselves in the flame of life. The name of this chakra is *Manipura*, which means "lustrous gem." This is the chakra of the solar plexus, of solar energy, of fire, of golden yellow light, shining with strength and will.

Fire

Our element is fire, and this chakra rules the *creation and expression of energy* in the body. Fire is the transformer, changing matter to energy in the form of heat and light. Whereas our first two chakras, earth and water, are subject to gravity, and flow downward, fire sends its heat and flames upward. This change is necessary for the transformational process of moving energy to the higher chakras. Physiologically this refers to metabolism, which changes our food and water into energy and heat. Psychologically, this relates to our expression of personal power and will, the actions created by the combination of body and movement from below, tempered by consciousness from above.

We can gain insight into the third chakra condition by examining our relationship to the metaphor of fire. Some of us have "warm" dispositions, while another's temperament may seem too hot. Others are cold, emotionally and/or physically. Some people have a style that is quick and energetic, while others are slow and lethargic. These are energetic styles, and may be relevant to several different chakras. We mention this here in the context of learning to examine the qualities of our own energetic style, and seeing its relationship to the element fire.

A healthy third chakra embodies a feeling of ease and warmth. There is laughter, pleasure, harmony with one's surroundings, and a joy in graceful and purposeful action. The power comes from within, and is neither oppressive nor submissive. It is not a power made of control, whether of self or others, but a power made of combination—mind and body, self and others, passion and compassion.

Power and Will

True power comes from the harmony of our polarities, much as electrical power comes from the combination of both positive and negative poles. Our personal power is greater when we combine both our male and female side, our light side and our shadow, our strength and vulnerability. Exploration of these polarities is the domain of chakra two. Combining them creates the power of chakra three.

If we look at the Chakra System as a whole, our power comes from the combination of the upward and downward current. The liberating current moving upward provides the energy, while the manifesting current moving downward from the consciousness of the upper chakras provides the form—channeling the energy much as wires channel electrical energy so that it may be used as power.

Consciousness, when applied to the fiery energy of chakra three, becomes *Will*. Will is the conscious direction of our life energy toward a manifest goal. Will is what differentiates raw energy from true power, for it is what guides, contains and harnesses that energy. To have strong will, we need consciousness— to *know* what our goals are, to have a conception in our mind of what we want to achieve. The instinctual energy of the first two chakras begins to change direction at this level, incorporating more consciousness into our actions and reactions.

A significant change of consciousness occurs when we shift our point of view from that of a victim to that of a co-creator. Victimization does exist and we have all had some experience as children in which we were victims. The recognition and mourning of this victimization is the emotional work of chakra two. However, if we continue to see our circumstances as someone else's fault, then we are powerless to change them. Moving into chakra three requires regarding our lives as a product of our own will, a difficult jump for many people to make. Only then do we really begin to connect with the power our personal will can truly have.

An appropriate concept to work with for the development of will is the Spiritual Warrior. This archetype represents one who is willing to stand their ground, to protect the sacred within, to accept challenges, and maintain power in a firm and quiet way. Good warriors radiate the sense that they are willing to fight bravely if they need to, and that very sense can keep a fight from occurring. Spiritual Warriors do not abuse their power, but operate within a context of strength, truth, and honor.

Power comes from the root *podere,* to be able. It is our task, in the third chakra, to reclaim our *right to act.* Reclaiming our right to act enables us to use our will, to begin a project and follow it through to the end, meeting the challenges we find; to take on a risk and not be bound by fear; and to lead without domination or aggrandizement. It enables us to confront without denial the injustices that occur and take action to set them right—making sure that we and others never become victims again.

Most of us suffer from what I call a "disabled will." Too many times we were made powerless, overly criticized or punished for our actions, taught to submit to authority, or taught that we were wrong, stupid, or bad. In this culture, we are raised to obedience. Parents teach children to suppress their anger, to never talk back even (and often especially) when there is abuse going on. Schools reward obedience, as do armies, and many jobs. Culturally we suffer from a disabled will. We pay taxes to finance wars we don't want, add to pollution while we commute to our jobs, submit ourselves daily to routines that suppress our spirit.

The disabled will is vulnerable to domination, for when we fail to realize our own will, others can use it instead. The army requires submission to authority which then directs the collective will to wield power against another force. Spouses, children, teachers or bosses can direct our will for us. The disabled will is vulnerable to addiction, to control by another, and to enslavement in general. When this happens, a feeling of powerlessness ensues, and the overall energy and vitality diminish, thus closing down the third chakra. A disabled will has no desire in it, and therefore no fire or enthusiasm.

It is through desire that we ignite the will. When we expand our horizons from self to other, from singleness to duality, we are given choice. To consciously choose is an act of will. Change and reorganization of our life energy are the result. Power, connected with our bodies and our feelings, and tempered through understanding, is the goal.

Excess and Deficiency

The physical task of the third chakra is to appropriately metabolize food into energy. Common malfunctions can manifest in many ways. Problems of digestion and metabolism, such as hypoglycemia or difficulty digesting foods signify too little energy, which is a deficiency. Diabetes or stomach ulcers are an "over-shooting" of metabolic functions, or an excessive reaction.

In general third chakra blockage can be seen as too much or too little energy. Addiction to substances that give the illusion of energy, such as caffeine, sugar, amphetamines or cocaine are the result of a basic deficiency in one's feeling of power and vitality. The substances give a temporary reprieve, but in the long run render an even greater deficiency, as they rob the body of health and rest. Chronic fatigue, an obvious third chakra deficiency, can be the result of addiction or disease. A weak immune system does not have the energy to "fight" disease. Rest and attention to diet are helpful for restoring deficient physical energy.

Obesity can be seen as a third chakra deficiency, because the body cannot appropriately metabolize the food into energy. (Obesity is a complex issue, however, that can involve more than one chakra.) Releasing third chakra blocks to expressing anger and reclaiming power can do wonders toward helping people regain balance in their weight.

Other physical characteristics reveal the state of the power center. A tight, hard stomach, (unless you're a weight lifter) indicates that power isn't flowing easily through your midsection—that there is constant tension or a need to defend. Sunken diaphragms, inability to get a deep breath through the belly, or "collapsed" third chakras, suggest a fear of taking power, of standing out, or sometimes of taking responsibility. These are all deficient characteristics.

Those with excessive third chakras may crave substances that sedate, such as alcohol, tranquilizers or opiates, because they soothe the hyperactive nervous system and bring a feeling of relaxation. An excessive third chakra can appear in what I call the "bully belly," an exaggerated puffiness around the middle that is not matched by relative amounts of weight in other areas, barring genetic factors. Those who have a strong need to be in control, to have power over others, to dominate, or to always appear superior are overcompensating for a damaged sense of their own true power.

Lack of self worth, or a hidden sense of shame, are usually found at the root of both excessive and deficient third chakra behaviors. Bringing consciousness to our roots, to our past, and working through our feelings are the methods of recovering from that shame and restoring the third chakra to its healthy role in the Chakra System— as a weaver of matter and consciousness into inner power.

Working with Movement

The goal in the third chakra is to bring attention to the solar plexus, the source of our energy. Some of these exercises activate the muscle groups that support this area of the body, while others involve using the solar plexus as the initiator, the source of the movements that radiate to other areas of the body. This chakra energizes and powers not just the solar plexus but the entire system, so we work with the body as a whole, directing you to walk and move with a variety of energy levels and styles. Let the walking exercises be an experiment to bring awareness of the patterns (habits) of moving that are familiar for you. Many of the exercises may introduce you to new and unfamiliar ways of feeling your strength and power. Incorporating these into your life, either as part of a movement practice or as something that you do throughout your day, allows you to experience that strength and power in ways that go beyond the physical, challenging your assumptions about what is possible for you in your life.

Walks

1 Feel your whole body, all the way from the connection of your feet with the ground, up through your legs, your hips, your torso, feeling each breath bringing energy into your body. When you feel grounded, begin to walk, using the entire space you have available. Walk with your normal walk, noticing how this feels, how your energy feels, how it is expressing itself in your walk. Notice what the third chakra area of your body feels like as you walk.

2 Now walk as if you are feeling very harried, very hassled, you've had a rough day, too much to do, you've got another three appointments and you're not sure you're going to get it all done, you have shopping to do, errands to run, and it's all too much, overwhelming. Notice the changes in your body as you're walking, feel the places where you tighten up, feel how your third chakra feels, then let that go.

3 Let your walk become aimless. You're not sure what you're doing today, you're not even sure what you're doing in this life. This walk has no purpose, no sense of direction. Again, feel how your body feels, feel how your third chakra feels. Notice the changes—how is this different from the harried, hassled walk? Again, let your walk change, this time into a purposeful walk, you know where you're going, you know you can get there, you know everything will turn out fine. You walk with a sense of direction, of purpose. Feel how your body feels, feel how your third chakra feels. Return to a neutral walk.

4 Now we'll try some walks that are less about your feeling state and more about your spatial and gravitational sense. Begin by letting your body become heavy, as if it has doubled in weight. Feel gravity pulling on you with every step that you take. Notice where in your body you feel that pull, where you feel that weight. How does it affect your body? How does your third chakra feel as you walk this way?

5 Let that weight lift from you and feel yourself lightening up, you almost have trouble not floating away, your body has become light as a feather, you are walking above the floor, weightless, as if gravity has disappeared. How does your body feel? How does your third chakra feel?

6 Find a balance between being weighted down and being so light you might float away, a place where you feel in balance. Notice how your body feels when you walk in a balanced way. Notice how your third chakra feels.

7 Now stop walking and feel the energy of your body in stillness. Bring your hand or hands to your third chakra to focus your attention there. Notice how your energy is moving through your body, which parts of you feel energized, which parts are not receiving any energy.

Boat Pose

1 Place yourself on your sitting bones with your knees bent and feet on the floor in front of you.

2 Lengthen your spine, allowing your torso to lean back as far as necessary to prevent your back from rounding.

3 On an exhalation, straighten one knee, extending your lower leg. Attempt to keep your upper leg in the position it was in with your knee bent. Be aware of the work in your abdominal muscles to keep your torso from falling back. Fold that leg back in and repeat with the other leg. These single leg extensions prepare you for the full boat pose, strengthening the muscles you'll need. Practice keeping your spine in alignment rather than collapsing it backwards, something which will be more difficult when you extend both legs.

4 For the full boat pose, extend both legs forward in the same manner that you extended the legs singly, then extend the arms forward, parallel to the floor, with palms facing towards each other, and shoulders sliding down away from your ears.

The Boat strengthens the muscles around the third chakra, and provides practice in working strongly while maintaining ease and relaxation in all the muscles that are not needed to create the pose.

Front Stretch

1 Start in the same position as the Boat pose, knees bent in front of you, feet on the ground. Place your hands behind you with fingers pointing down towards your feet.

2 On an exhalation, straighten your arms and legs, pressing your hip sockets up towards the ceiling. Imagine your front hip bones lifting up towards your head as your tailbone reaches down towards your toes. Contract your buttocks and lengthen your spine as your shoulders pull down away from your ears. This pose combines strength with the opening of the front of the body, especially the solar plexus.

Transition through Squat

From the front stretch bring your buttocks back down to the floor, bend your knees and pull your feet in. Use your hands on the floor to press your center of balance forward onto your feet, then move your hands to balance over your feet. Roll up to standing in the same way as in the first chakra (p. 55).

Vibration

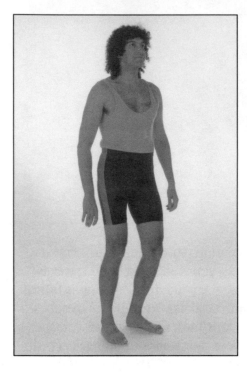

Sink your feet into the earth and imagine them as part of the earth, growing out of the earth. Feel your roots extending down from your feet and let those roots begin to dance with the soil around them. Feel the movement of root tendrils dancing with the moisture in the soil, dancing with the deep humming energy of this living, moving planet. As the dance of your roots progresses, the energy begins to move up into your feet and legs, and your muscles respond by slightly bending your knees rhythmically, alternating legs to create a pumping feeling. Your knees don't bend very much and never straighten to the point of tightening. Your heels barely lift off the ground. Breathe easily and deeply, feeling your breath fill your lungs. Your body, including the upper torso, neck, head, and arms, hangs easily, allowing the breath to move through it. The vibration moves up through your legs, bouncing through your pelvis and traveling up through your spine (and through your chakras), awakening all the cells, all the muscles as they are shaken by the movement and the energy pumping up through you by the action of your knees and feet.

Use music that is rhythmic and percussive enough to inspire energetic movement. Match your knee movements to the rhythm of the music. Make sure that the music you are using allows you to pump at a pace that is comfortable for you to maintain your synchronization with its rhythm.

Now bring the rest of your body into the movement, allowing the shaking and vibrating that has been traveling up your legs and into your torso to move its focus to other parts of your body. Imagine that there is a ball of energy moving through you and as it travels through each part of your body it shakes and vibrates that energy into movement. Play with it, feel it like flames dancing in the space that your body occupies, flames that originate from a bright, shining, sparkling sun right at your solar plexus.

Spinal Axis Movement

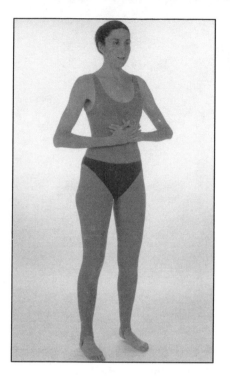

As you continue to vibrate energy up and through your legs and pelvis, place your hands on your solar plexus. Feel the vibration under your palms and visualize a growing sphere of yellow pulsing under your hands, a small sun generating energy from this center out to the rest of your body. In particular, pay attention to the energy as it flows through your torso and into your shoulders and out your arms.

Now, as you begin to move your solar plexus in space (with the rest of your body following along), allow the flow of its movement to travel out into the arms, a flaming river of energy moving from within your center and out through hands and fingers to rejoin the energies that swirl around in the space that you're in.

Begin to cover space with this movement, traveling around the room with your third chakra, your solar plexus leading the movement, generating energy that radiates from that center up the spine. Without bending the spine, allow it to twist to allow the movement to flow out the arms. In more mundane terminology—your spine maintains its alignment while your torso and arms twist and spiral around it. Let the movement wind down to stillness and experience the energy moving through you as you stand still.

Woodchopper

The Woodchopper provides practice in gathering the energy of the body and releasing it. As you bring your whole being into the movement and sound, you may be amazed at the strength and energy you have within you. This is especially useful if you who are shy and have difficulty being visibly powerful in the world.

1 Plant your feet firmly in the ground, about two feet apart. Keep your knees slightly bent. Raise your arms over your head, hands clasped together. Reach up and slightly back as you inhale.

2 Descend swiftly on an exhalation, letting out a loud "ahh" sound as your torso swings down, chopping between your legs. Repeat several times, allowing the movement of your body and the sound you make to be as full as possible.

Making the Sun

1 Stand with your feet parallel, hip width apart, arms down at your sides. Imagine lifting up, growing from roots that sink deep into the ground from your feet. Resting your pelvis gently on the tops of your thigh bones, visualize your spine growing up towards the sky. Your shoulders drop down away from your ears and your neck lengthens as the top of your head (the crown) lifts up. Your arms lengthen down towards the ground, not tensing, but reaching.

2 Keep lengthening and reaching with your arms as you slowly lift them out to the side, creating the widest arc you can.

3 At shoulder height remember to drop your shoulders down again if they have lifted, and turn your palms over to face up.

4 Continue the journey of your arms up towards the sky. (Once you have the idea, you'll want to complete the arc from bottom to top with one inhalation of breath.) Turn your palms over again, facing them out, and with an exhalation slowly lower them back down, pressing through the space around you with the energy of the sun's rays. Imagine yourself the sun, energy running through you and out your arms. When your arms have completed their circuit, feel the solar glow that you have created around you.

Warrior

Stand with your feet parallel, about four or five feet apart. Turn your right leg out 90 degrees so that your toes and knee are facing to the right side. Turn your left leg slightly in towards center. Lengthen your arms down at your sides and slowly raise them to shoulder height, reaching out to either side as your shoulders drop down away from your ears and your neck lengthens. Maintain the position of your right leg and at the same time turn your torso to face as much as possible towards the front. Turn your head to look out along your right arm. Take a deep breath in and as you exhale slowly bend your right knee over your foot, attempting to form a right angle with your thigh and your calf, with your knee directly over your heel. Keep your torso upright and centered, not leaning out over your right leg or backwards towards your left leg. Keep your left leg straight, contracting the thigh muscle to lift the kneecap. When you feel finished, slowly straighten your right knee as you inhale, bringing yourself back up and then switching leg positions to repeat on the other side.

Practicing the Warrior pose, in addition to developing strength and stamina, provides practice in finding the balance between aggression (pushing too far towards the bent front leg) and withdrawal from a challenge (pulling back away from the front leg, sinking onto the back leg). The Warrior stands ready, centered, expending only the energy that is necessary to maintain that ready state, not wasting energy in aggression.

The Dance

The movements of the third chakra are an expression of your strength and power, your right to take up space in the world. This is an assertive dance, with movements that announce your presence and your right to be here. Often the dance is expansive, so make sure you have enough space to move without feeling constricted. Let your movements express your largeness, your sureness, your energy. You may start from the fiery movement of Vibration, letting the energy generated take on a life of its own in your body. Perhaps your dance starts in the firm, steady, strength of the Warrior, with slow, sweeping movements that define your boundaries and exhibit your confidence. The Woodchopper could start your dance by filling your space with sound and the swift, strong assertion of your body chopping down through space and then swinging in other directions as the energy moves you. You may choose to begin with the concepts and images that come to mind for the third chakra and allow them to take form in your body, with no preconceived idea of what that should look like—this is your dance, dance it with all your might!

Partner Work: Space Invasion

Stand facing your partner, two or three feet apart. One of you attempts to invade the space of the other, while the invaded partner protects himself from invasion. Change roles to give each a chance to invade and be invaded. How well do you maintain your power while protecting your boundaries?

Partner Work: Towel Pull

Stand about three feet apart, each of you holding the end of a towel. Without moving your feet, play tug of war with the towel, each of you attempting to pull the towel away from the other. Feel free to let the little kid inside you yell things like "Mine!" "Gimme!" This helps us connect to the "will stage" of our childhood and access the feelings that were developing at that time.

Partner Work: Statues

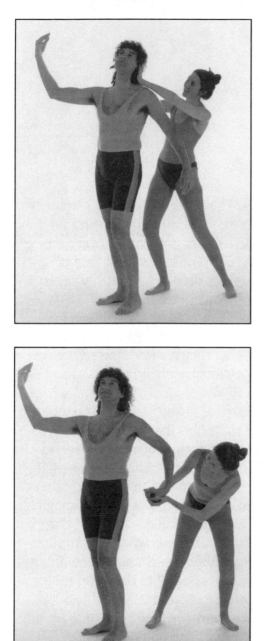

One partner becomes the sculptor while the other stands in a neutral position, ready to be sculpted. The sculptor moves the neutral body into whatever interesting position they like, while the statue holds the position the sculptor puts them in. When the sculptor is done, the statue maintains the pose for long enough to appreciate how it feels, then changes the pose in some way to make it more their own, reclaiming the body and its pose. Try several poses before changing roles.

This exercise often brings up issues of control, as each partner surrenders to the whims of the other. The choices we make as we move through our lives may be dictated by others without our even noticing that we have surrendered to the will of the media or our parents or peer group or any number of outside forces. Being molded so overtly by another provides an opportunity to observe this process and then to reclaim ourselves as we reclaim the pose by choosing how we want it to be.

Putting It Into Practice

Taking risks

Power and will are like muscles. They seldom get stronger when idle. If we always stick to what's safe and sure (first chakra function) then we don't get the experience of growing, of overcoming, of being triumphant and feeling our power. We don't gain confidence without taking risks. The risks need to be sensibly calculated however, as failure does little to build confidence.

Risks can take many forms. Some people take physical risks, experimenting with parachute jumping, hang-gliding, surfing, or even just pushing the edges of what they believe their physical limitations to be. Other risks may involve saying things to someone that you've been afraid to say, such as a confrontation where you ask for what you want or practice saying "no" for a change.

What risks could you take right now that you have been avoiding? Experience what happens in your solar plexus as you imagine approaching the risk, engaging in it, and completing it. What has kept you from doing this, what are the fears and other feelings that arise when you imagine it? It might help to imagine also how you will respond to the imagined consequences. For example, run through in your mind what you will say to the person with whom you've been avoiding a particular issue. Imagine their response, and how you will respond to that. You might want to role-play this dialogue with a supportive friend to allow you to practice. Now go do it, and compare how your solar plexus feels in actuality. Compare your projection and the reality.

Breaking inertia

Freeing up energy is a matter of breaking inertia. Blocks hold on as much by habit as anything else. If you feel stuck and can't get loose, go running, play at having a fit, get moving, do anything safe to overcome the inertia. Once you have some momentum going, then you have energy to work with and it is easier to do whatever you decide is important. Some of the physical exercises described in the movement section for this chakra are especially good for this. *Do something very active once a day.*

Examine Energy Systems

You are a complete energy system. You are also part of several larger energy systems—your family, your workplace, your community, culture, and country. Since the third chakra deals with energetic dynamics, it is a good idea to examine your various energy systems for dysfunctions. Typical energetic dysfunctions are:

- Imbalances of power, such as needing to be in control, or being submissive. Who in your immediate energy web has these problems and how do they affect you?

- Imbalances in work output, such as taking on more of a particular kind of work in a system. This could be emotional work, communication work, initiatory work (getting things started), actual work (as in overtime, extra commitment), caretaking work, parenting, or housework.

- Blocks in the system. Where does energy traveling through the system typically get hung up? What are the forces acting on this person or element of the system? What can be done to help the energy flow more smoothly?

Take some steps to change these energy systems if they need it, by changing your own energetic approach.

Resistance

Here we look at where we experience the most resistance in our energy field. Maybe we have difficulty getting things started, maybe we resist confrontation, maybe we resist intimacy. In examining resistance, it is important to validate why the resistance is there. We cannot merely bulldoze over it. Resistance disappears faster when we can get at the reason for it, acknowledge it, and compensate for it by responding to the need in a healthier way. If you don't know why you have resistance to a particular thing, ask your inner child. He or she probably knows.

What do you often resist? What are you afraid of? Where does the fear come from? What can you do to make it feel less threatening, or to be better able to meet the risk?

Take some steps to remove the resistance. Try doing your task without giving in to resistance (use your will).

Passion, Will, and Breaking Attachments

These may seem like contradictions, but they are all relevant to the third chakra. Our passion gives fuel and zest to the will. When our feelings are dulled, our will has no enthusiasm—it becomes a rigid structure, rather than focused energy. This is how the second chakra serves the third—by revealing our feelings, desires and passions.

If, however, our passions become fixated on something that is not manifesting, or something that is not healthy for us (like a destructive relationship, for example), then we can free up an enormous amount of energy by letting go of that attachment. This ties in with the examination of energy systems above. If your attachment is not serving your energy system in a positive way then you are depleting your power and undermining the development of your third chakra. Take some steps to break attachments that are not serving your energy system.

Higher power

One of the important principles of recovery programs is surrendering to a "higher power." In terms of chakras, when we open to a "higher" power, we are opening to the power of the chakras above us. As we open to our high self, we bring down consciousness through the crown chakra, to feed and energize all the chakras below.

We can also open to a "deeper" power. This is opening to the power of the earth, the power of our bodies and our feelings. When we mix these two powers together, we are bridging a polarity and enhancing the power of our lives.

Do a meditation using each of these powers as an aid in your daily life. Try them alone, or in combination, and compare how they make you feel and how they aid you in your problems.

Running energy

You are made up of energy. The third chakra is seen as a generator and distributor of that energy.

A good meditation to do each day is to sit quietly and simply feel this energy. Feel where it is strongest and weakest and in what direction it wants to move. Then allow yourself to visualize and imagine kinesthetically the feeling of the energy running down from the top of the crown, imagining that you are taking it in from the sun, sky and stars above. Run it down through your body, through each chakra, pouring it into the third chakra, and then down through your lower chakras into your ground. When you get to the bottom, go up and run it through again and again until it seems to run smoothly, letting all tension drain out the bottom.

When this downward current runs smoothly, do the same thing with the upward current, pulling energy up from the earth and running it through your legs, into your first chakra, up through all the chakras and out through the crown at the top of your head.

Think of this as combing through the aura, much as we comb through our hair to get the tangles out. This process of getting everything to go in one direction magnetizes our energy field, much as we magnetize a nail when we stroke it in one direction with a magnet.

Think of the downward current as going down the front of the body, and the upward current as rising up the spine, though this is not a hard and fast rule. Following these pathways, the two currents form a continuous circuit of energy rather than crossing each other.

Putting yourself out in the world

Write political action letters about issues that concern you to your representatives or to a corporation engaging in behavior you disapprove of. Write a letter to the editor of your newspaper about an issue you have thoughts or feelings about. Make your will known in the world and take action.

Experiment with changing your behavior regarding leadership in the groups you belong to. If you are always the one to take a powerful role, try encouraging others to do so while you follow this time. If you wait for others to lead, try stepping forward to take the reins.

Towel Squeeze

Take a towel and fold it several times so that you can grab it like a tube and twist it. Think of something that makes you angry and twist the towel, projecting your anger into your activity. Count to ten and then stop. After regaining your composure, twist the towel again. Alternate between these two stages until you feel you have a sense of balancing the control and the release of your anger.

Anger

Anger is a release and expression of power. Used wisely and carefully, a good, healthy expression of anger, safely delivered, can be of immense help in unblocking the power chakra. This can be done alone, or with the help of a friend or therapist.

Get grounded first, and have something soft that can be hit or pushed against. Use a large plastic bat to hit against a mat on the floor. The mat also can stand upright, folded, and act as a punching bag.

Using the bat may feel mechanical to some people at first, but if you stick with it you may find another kind of energy starts to surface. Getting this energy to release in a safe way decreases the probability that it will release inadvertently on friends and loved ones. (We do not recommend this exercise if you are prone to rage already. If you feel the exercise might open areas you would have a hard time controlling, get a trusted friend or therapist to help you proceed slowly. The exercise at left is a good place to start.)

Laughter

While tears are part of the emotional expression of the second chakra, laughter comes straight from the solar plexus. When we can laugh at something, it no longer has power over us.

Try to pick an aspect of yourself that you have trouble accepting. Close your eyes and imagine watching yourself engage in this trait, as if you were watching from a place on another plane, high above. See if you can move from judgment to a feeling of amusement as you watch this behavior. In short, laugh at yourself.

Once can you do this with one of your own traits, try it with a trait of a friend or partner that you have equal difficulty with. Again, try to move from judgment to amusement as you look at them engaging in this behavior.

Play

Children love to use their energy in a physical way at play. With a child, or with an adult friend who is willing to play, allow the playful child to come out in you. Take a trip to a playground and play on the equipment, run in the grass, tackling your friend and being tackled. Within the constraints of your furniture, play on the rug at home, tussling, rolling, tickling.

Journal Exercises

1. Power

The main issue of the third chakra is the examination and development of our personal power. The following questions help to bring this issue into focus.

• What, to you, constitutes power?

• How do you know when you have it?

• How do you know when someone else has it?

• When do you feel most powerful?

• When do you feel least powerful?

• If you think of yourself as developing personal power, what do you want that power for? What do you want to do with it?

• Who in your life (past or present) do you think of as being powerful in a way that you respect? What is it about this person that makes this so?

• How are you affected by their power?

• How do they behave to give this sense of power?

2. Will and Goals

The first step in developing a stronger will is to validate your present will by seeing that your will creates everything you do and have. This is even true if it's something you think you don't want to do—it is still your will that directs it. Only when we realize that the will is quite operative can we learn to redirect it.

It is hard to activate will without a purpose or goal. Without these, will becomes merely whim. Relevance to overall purpose is a valuable barometer for distinguishing between will and whim.

Journal Exercises

Make a list of your goals and purposes for the week. At the end of the week examine how many of them got done and how many you bypassed.

- What stopped you? What distracted you?

- Did you list too many? Are they really your priorities?

- How would you rate the ability of your will to carry through?

Make a list of goals and purposes you want to accomplish over the next five years.

- How many of your daily actions are relevant to the fulfillment of these purposes?

- How do you get waylaid off your path?

- What parts are hardest to fulfill?

- What are the messages that get in the way?

- What is blocking your will?

Think about what you would like to accomplish in your lifetime. Make a list of these overall goals.

- Are your five year goals in line with your overall goals?

- Are your weekly goals in line with your overall goals?

3. Reassessment

- What have you learned about yourself as you've worked through the activities for the third chakra?

- What areas of this chakra do you need to work on? How will you do that?

- What areas do you feel pleased with? How can you utilize these strengths?

Entering Sacred Space

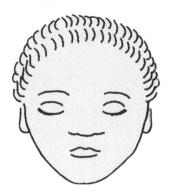

Candle meditation

Since the element of this chakra is fire, a candle flame as a visual focus is an appropriate meditation tool. You can do a nightly meditation on this flame (best done in the dark, but not crucial). Seat yourself comfortably in front of the candle and let your gaze rest softly upon the flame. Feel your solar plexus and imagine that this flame burns there as well, allowing the two to connect. Feel the warmth and let the image of the fire "burn" its way into your consciousness until you can close your eyes and still retain a vivid image of the flame. Now think of the word or words written on your candle (from the group ritual) and imagine them burning in front of you. Let the fire of that purpose come into you, imagining the flame igniting your will to begin and complete your stated purpose. Bring that into your third chakra and let its energy move from there throughout your whole body. To this, you may wish to add the Breath of Fire exercise below.

Breath of Fire

This is a rapid diaphragmatic breathing from the yoga tradition of pranayama. Sit comfortably with your back aligned and take a deep breath. When the breath is full, pull your diaphragm in suddenly so that the breath rushes out through your nose in a sharp burst. Then relax your diaphragm, and you will find your breath naturally fills again by itself. When it is again full, snap the diaphragm again, and repeat over and over again. At first you will want to do it slowly, so that you get the feel of it. Once that happens you can work on doing it faster and faster. The speed, however, is not as important as doing the exercise correctly.

Group Ritual
Materials Needed

Candle and candleholder for each participant
A piece of paper and pen for each participant
Cauldron or fireplace
Spicy food and beverages

Preparation

With a pen or other sharp instrument, write on the candle a word
or two that signifies an essential goal for you right now, such as
healing, losing weight, or finishing a project.

Creating Sacred Space

All participants enter the ritual space with a sense of their
strength, chanting the syllable of the third chakra, Ram, as they
move throughout the space, defining their boundaries. They place
their candles on the altar in the center and form a circle around it.

Invoking the Directions

Call each of the four quarters by invoking the following power
animals or others with whom you feel more in tune.

> *South—lion*
> *West—whale*
> *North—bull*
> *East—hawk*

Reclaiming Power

Write on a piece of paper the name of a person, thing or situation
that you hold responsible for something in your life, to whom you
have relinquished your power in some way. One at a time participants come to the cauldron or fireplace and burn the piece of
paper, saying aloud or silently who or what it is that they release
from blame. They take their candle, engraved with their goals and
purpose, and light it from the flames of the burning paper, stating
that they take back their power from this person or thing and now
dedicate it to achieving their goals.

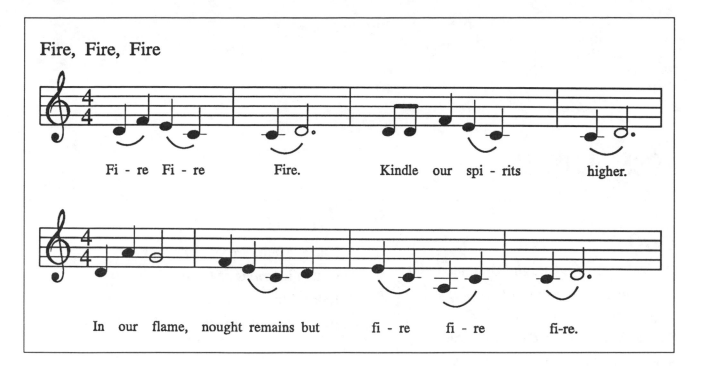

Fire, Fire, Fire

Fi - re Fi - re Fire. Kindle our spi - rits higher.

In our flame, nought remains but fi - re fi - re fi-re.

Chant

This can be sung softly as the pieces of paper are burned, or afterwards, while Making the Sun.

Fire, fire, fire song. (see above)

Making the Sun

Standing in a circle, all perform this pose together, visualizing their own individual sun and a larger, stronger sun comprised of the joined energies of the group, giving support and power to the working just finished.

Communion

All share spicy food and beverages (as symbolic of fire).

Grounding

Ground the energy and open the circle, each participant taking their candle home with them to burn during meditation.

Resources

Books

Harvey, Bill. *Mind Magic*. Unlimited Pub.

Macy, Joanna. *Despair & Personal Power in the Nuclear Age*. New Society Pub.

Starhawk, *Dreaming the Dark*. Beacon.

Starhawk, *Truth or Dare*. Harper & Row.

von Oech, Roger. *Creative Whack Pack*. (deck of cards). U.S. Games Systems.

Music

Isham, Mark. *Vapor Drawings*.

Olatunji. *Drums of Passion*.

Reich, Steve. *Drumming*.

Roach, Steve. *Traveler*.

Chakra Four

Heart

Getting Started

Where Are You Now?

Take time to reflect on the following concepts and write down whatever thoughts or phrases come to mind about how these concepts operate in your life.

Balance	*Receiving*
Love	*Breath*
Compassion	*Affinity*
Relationship	*Grace*
Openness	*Equilibrium*
Giving	*Peace*

This chakra involves the heart, the upper chest and the upper back. How do you feel about these areas of your body? Are there any difficulties you've had in these areas at any time during your life?

Altar Arrangement

The fourth chakra centers on the themes of love and compassion, as well as the element of air. Feathers and fans are appropriate as symbols of air, and pictures of flying creatures. Use fragrances and incense on the altar to stimulate the awareness of breath. Photographs of those you love and hold dear can mingle with airy pictures. Any symbols that you associate with love, or pictures of people who you see as especially compassionate would go well on your altar. A green altar cloth and candle are appropriate and perhaps an image of Quan Yin or another deity of compassion.

Correspondences

Sanskrit name	Anahata
Meaning	Sound that is made without any two things striking, unstruck
Location	Heart
Element	Air
Main Issue	Love, relationships
Goals	Balance in relationships and with self, compassion, self-acceptance
Malfunction	*Deficient:* isolation, low self-esteem, collapsed chest, shallow breathing, melancholy. *Excessive:* codependent care-taking, clinging behaviors
Color	Green
Planet	Venus
Foods	Vegetables
Right	To Love
Stones	Emerald, rose quartz
Animals	Antelope, dove
Operating principle	Equilibrium
Yoga Path	Bhakti Yoga (devotional yoga)
Archetype	Aphrodite, Quan Yin, Christ

Sharing the Experience

"Last month I was stuck in the first chakra, which has improved somewhat. Now I feel more stable. But I've had a lot of pain in my heart chakra this last month. I need to solve these old childhood issues, but I've been able to deal with it without taking it out on my boyfriend. I feel like I'm making progress healing my inner child, and that has a lot to do with my heart. I'm beginning to feel contentment, like I've gotten lighter. It's not exactly how I'd like it to be, but it's moving in the right direction."

•

"My body has been doing weird things. At the beginning of the month my chest was hurting so bad it was as if someone was sitting on it. It was a part of me that I hadn't accepted or loved in myself. I did some healing work on it and it was like I could barely breathe and then all of a sudden it just exploded and my whole heart opened up. Since then, the energy in my body has been coming up through my feet, I can feel it, and my sensation is heightened everywhere, but especially in the lower body which I usually don't feel. My vision's increasing—I am having psychic experiences. Everything's opened up and it's coming really quickly. I guess I opened up my Kundalini energy."

•

"Well, an interesting month. Circumstances have been going to my core issues around the fourth chakra and bringing stuff up. It's been very painful. Bringing up denial and confusion. My heart's felt pressured, and it feels empty, like something that's not going on there. I feel like I'm getting better at communicating with myself, listening inside."

•

"I started the month becoming aware of a tear between my heart and my soul, recognizing that there was a real separation for me. I think that this month I have become aware of the holes in my heart—there's fullness around but the holes are there. I've had to come to terms with feeling lonely."

•

"When we ended last session I thought this fourth chakra was going to be easy stuff. What I found is that it is not so easy. A lot of stuff is coming up around relationships. My ex-lover wants us to get back together. I had to say no. We're real busy working and giving and loving other people, but I am not having time for my own current relationship. But me and my lover are closer than we ever have been and we're going to find time to be with each other."

•

"For me the fourth chakra has been finding a source in self-love. I feel like finally in this round I got one of life's giant lessons. And what I found was that in doing something out of the act of love for myself, it wasn't greed, it wasn't any of those parts at all, this was 100% for me, and I was just in an easy state of self-love. It just sat there strong and clear. And in doing that, all the other chakras just lined up. The first chakra brought me all kinds of abundance, and the second chakra opened up incredible vibration of that, and old lovers returned, and I could say all the things I needed to say, from this centered place of self-love. There was no aggression. Also I quit smoking—which has happened many times with failure, but this time I had such acceptance that I don't want to smoke, there's just no desire, and it feels permanent. It feels different—my breath is open, my heart is open."

•

"My sweetie and I celebrated our first month together and we're dealing with all seven chakras. The fourth chakra has been coming up. Last fall I asked to open up my heart. What I've been going through with this new relationship has fun parts and scary parts. The fun parts everybody knows. The scary parts are the nightmares I have every once in a while that the relationship will be devastated. I know it's just my fear, left over from past relationships that haven't lasted. But this time it feels so right, I know I can't walk away from it, and I've managed to keep the heart chakra open, even in my fear."

"I thought this would be a month of sweetness and light, but it wasn't. I cried a lot this month. I discovered I can't say 'I love you,' as easily as some people. I became aware of my own tendency to judge. And I thought how that wasn't very loving and took it on to replace judgment with compassion. I worked on creating balance in my family with my husband, as his traveling changes the balance in the whole family system every time he comes and goes."

•

"The fourth chakra was really heavy, real physical for me. I could feel my heart—a lot of irregular beating, a lot of intensity, trouble breathing. That was in the beginning of the month, and within one week it was like I had a lot of very emotional results with friends who came back to talk, telling me how they missed me and loved me, and that was overwhelming. I learned about compassion. I focused on the irregularity of my heart beat and focused then on my first chakra—about the heaviness of my body, and it brought me out of denial, that I need to take action about lightening my body. In order to function properly, I realized I have to release—love, power, energy, etc. The fourth made me realize I had work to do on the other chakras. But strange people brought me flowers and were good to me and I was appreciative and felt humbled that the universe had opened up for me, to help me love myself and accept other people's love for me."

Understanding the Concept

We now enter the very center of the Chakra System. With three chakras below and three chakras above, chakra four lies literally at the heart of the whole system. Known as the "heart" chakra, because it is located in the area of that vital organ, this center is at the core of our spirit. In many languages, the word for heart comes from the root for core, as in the French *coeur*, and the Spanish *corazon*. And in our language, to go to the heart of an issue is to get to the core. One of the many pathways of energy through the chakras is a spiral, emanating from the heart, as the core, and traveling through each of the chakras in ever expanding pairs. (See illustration, pg. 185.)

Chakra four is the ceiling of the lower world and the root of the upper world. For this reason it is a point of balance, the integrator between the worlds of spirit and matter. The symbol of the heart chakra is a lotus of twelve petals, within which lies a six-pointed star. This is the *trikona* (triangle of energy) of spirit descending towards matter, and the trikona of matter arising towards spirit. The six-pointed star expresses their interpenetration in perfect balance.

Air

The heart chakra is the center of *love, compassion, balance,* and *peace.* Its element is *air,* the lightest element thus far. Air is the element of the breath, of the oxygen pumped through our bloodstream with every heartbeat. The lungs, as they fill and empty with air, are like branches and tendrils of the heart chakra. The cells of the heart beat in unison, and continue unceasing from within the womb, throughout our entire life. When we work with air, as we interact with it through the breath, we have access to the physical and spiritual aspects of the heart chakra. This practice is called *pranayama,* from the Hindu word for breath as *prana,* or first unit. Pranayama is the yoga of breathing exercises, the process of nourishing the body and mind with the vital energy of the breath. Opening up the breath, relaxing the muscles of the chest, and listening to the beat of the heart help us to enter the sacred precinct of the heart chakra.

Air expands, caresses, and energizes. It fills any space it enters, yet is soft and gentle. Like water, air takes the shape of that which it fills, but it is lighter and less subject to gravity. With the heat of the third chakra below it, air may even rise. If I light a stick of incense in the room, the smell spreads more or less evenly throughout the room over time, demonstrating the sense of evenness, of equilibrium in the quality of air. So too with love.

Love

Love is the basic principle associated with the heart chakra. Love is the expansive state of spirit, the transcendence of boundaries and limitations, the interconnectedness and meeting point of interpenetrating planes. Love in the fourth chakra is felt as a state of being, emanating from the center and radiating out to all that it encounters. It is not dependent on an object, as the passionate nature of the second chakra might be, but exists within the individual as an independent state and spreads to all that it encounters. Fueled by the fires of passion and will below, it is an uplifting energy, opening us to the expansion of spirit characteristic of the chakras that dwell above.

The Sanskrit name for this chakra is *Anahata*, which means *sound that is made without any two things striking*, or unstruck, unhurt. This is the peaceful balance of the heart, where the fight of the third chakra has turned to graceful acceptance in the fourth. If the will has done its job, then we have arranged our lives so that we are in our "proper place," and we can relax and accept, allow, open and receive. This is the meaning implied by the magical maxim of Aleister Crowley: "Love is the Law, Love under Will." Only when our will has done its job can it truly let go and allow us to enter the state of trust and balance of the heart chakra.

Equilibrium and Balance

Each chakra has a basic principle that governs its energetic pattern; the principle of *equilibrium* governs the heart chakra. That which has equilibrium has longevity—the balanced relationship lasts. When we truly enter into balance with ourselves, our relationships, and our environment, we enter a deep sense of serenity and peace. This is a *dynamic* equilibrium—one that balances out over time, giving each person room to fluctuate within the relationship. One of the tasks of the heart chakra is to move into a state of balance with all around us, letting our own heart beat in unison with the heartbeat of the web of life, through which we are intricately connected. We then have the balance of the universe to assist and guide us in all that we do.

Love is an interpenetration of energy fields, much as the two intersecting triangles in the lotus describe. This implies relationship, be it a relationship between different aspects of ourselves, spirit and matter, a mother and child, culture and environment, or one lover to another. Without an overall sense of balance, however, a relationship breaks down. It is through balance that love is sustained.

This is particularly true in our relationships with others. If Mary is always doing the initiating, or the cleaning, or the emotional processing for the relationship, there is an apparent lack of balance. In time, she will tire of this imbalance and look for other relationships in which she experiences a greater equality. There is always some balance in any relationship that endures, however, even relationships that seem to be oppressive. Mary might choose to stay in the relationship because she appreciates financial support or because her mate offers her something else in return that she is unable to provide for herself.

Healthy relationships seek a healthy balance, a voluntary balance. The sound that is made without any two things striking comes from a voluntary giving of energy to another, and a giving that is met voluntarily on the other side. If a person is put in the position of having to provide more than they receive in a relationship, feelings of obligation and resentment set in, and these are the enemies of love. While outer circumstances of a relationship might bind us, such as children or housing situations, true heart chakra commitment comes from a balanced meeting of needs, desires, and challenges.

Self-love is an important element in achieving this balance. It is difficult to enter into love with another if we don't establish self-love first. In other words, we need to be somewhat balanced within ourselves. This rests on an understanding and acceptance of our personal dualities—a balance between shadow and light, inner and outer, giving and receiving, adult and inner child—and a willingness to listen to our needs and respond to them. When in balance, we enter a state of grace. When another loves us, it is somehow easier to love ourselves, but if we are dependent upon this for self-love, we are threatening a healthy balance once again.

Reflective Consciousness

At the heart chakra we enter into "self-reflective" consciousness. The lower chakras run largely on instinct, and their consciousness orientation may be beyond our control, such as the survival mechanisms that kick in when we are threatened, or the overwhelming feelings we may experience in some situations.

Here at the heart center we are less reactive and more contemplative. We experience events in terms of relationships—how one thing relates to another. Our experience of the relationships *between* things is more important than the things themselves.

Excess & Deficiency

If the heart chakra energy is deficient, one can feel a sense of pressure over the sternum, and getting a deep breath may be difficult without effort. The chest may appear collapsed and there is a tendency toward depression. A person with this condition may choose isolation, fear interpersonal relationships, or simply suffer from a lack of self-esteem. With the heart chakra closed down, the very core of the chakra system is depressed, and it is difficult for energy to pass between the upper and lower body. There may even be a profound mind-body split. Conditions such as this may be the result of neglect or abandonment, emotional abuse, or shaming experiences from childhood. In adulthood, the accumulation of unshed grief weighs heavy on the heart chakra and often suppresses the breath and the natural expansion of the chest.

If the heart chakra is excessive, or open without boundaries, there is a tendency to give everything away, to be so focused on others that we ignore the core self—the profile of a codependent personality. Here we are not operating from within our own center, but living through others. Causes for this condition may be very similar to the causes for a deficient heart chakra. Whether one chooses the defense of isolation and withdrawal or overactivity influences the way in which the energy passes through the heart chakra into the outside world of interpersonal relationships. Again our goal is a healthy balance.

Universal love

The concept of universal love is the spiritual value behind the heart chakra. Universal love is the ability to enter into appropriate and meaningful relationship with our environment, to experience compassion and connection with all that surrounds us, and to be able to maintain our own centers while remaining open and connected. Compassion comes through the understanding of patterns—the ability to see the forces that acted upon a person or situation to shape their patterns. When we are centered and clear about our own patterns, it is easier to have compassion for others.

In summary, the task of the heart chakra is to enter into a state of balance within ourselves and in our relationships and to open compassion and love. The passage of energy through the heart connects mind and body, inner and outer, self and other, and rewards us with a profound sense of peace and fulfillment.

Working with Movement

Bringing one's life into balance and maintaining that balance is not about staying still. Just as balancing a scale requires making adjustments in weight on one side of the scale to counterbalance whatever weight is placed on the other side, balance in life requires making appropriate adjustments in response to new challenges or information. Learning to make these adjustments smoothly—without overreacting and then having to recover from that excess of response—helps maintain a healthy equilibrium.

It's important to realize that, when we perform any of the poses or movements in this book, the work is not just in the "final" pose or static position that we attain at the peak. The process of opening and closing is as much a part of the practice of these exercises as the specified goal pose. To finish any pose, come down slowly rather than dropping out of it into collapse. If you think to yourself, "OK, I've gotten there, I've done it, now it's over and I can let go of it and just drop myself to the floor," you are missing half the exercise, which is to learn to make transitions gently and allow yourself to flow into and out of the poses.

There is a hierarchy of stretch, in that certain muscles in any given pose are the first layer, and we need to stretch them out before we can stretch the next layer down. Often, we chose an exercise for a particular chakra less for its direct effect on the specific area of the body, and more for its ability to open up related areas. These areas often collapse around the chakra area, keeping us from stimulating that area.

Much of the movement work of the fourth chakra works on opening up forward-rounded shoulders and tight shoulders, which allows for the eventual opening up of a collapsed chest and the stimulation of the heart area. As you perform these exercises, keep this in mind, and maintain your awareness of the heart opening as you release the surrounding areas that keep it constricted.

Wall Hang

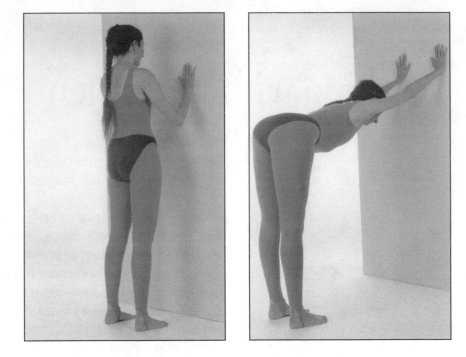

1 Stand facing the wall, about six inches away, and place your hands parallel and flat against the wall at shoulder height and shoulder width apart.

2 Step back away from the wall, placing the feet parallel and hip width apart. How far from the wall you step will depend on how tall you are and how flexible you are. The taller and/or more tight you are, the further you need to be, the shorter and/or more flexible, the closer.

Imagine your body as two sections—your legs from the top of the thigh down, and your torso, head and arms, from the sitting bones up. Tilt the pelvis forward and pull the sitting bones up towards the ceiling and back away from the wall.

For fourth chakra effects we will focus on the opening in the upper body, but notice also the sensations in the backs of your legs as you move into this pose, because maintaining straight legs will stretch the hamstrings. The important effect here for our purposes is that the upper chest and armpit area stretches open. Relax into this stretch, continuing to breathe easily and imagining your spine lengthening and your heart area opening.

Couch Stretch

Sit down with your upper back to the arm of a couch, lift your arms up and over backwards over the side of the couch and let them hang back. Focus on relaxing, releasing to the weight of your arms and head, and allowing your heart area to stretch open.

Over Head Stretch

1 Hold a belt with both hands, leaving three to four feet between your hands and stretching the belt taut.

2 Keeping your elbows straight, lift your arms forward and up over your head.

3 Let your hands slide only as far apart as is absolutely necessary to allow your arms to go over and behind you. Leave your hands where they are on the belt as you raise your arms back up and over to the front.

Face Down Chest Openings

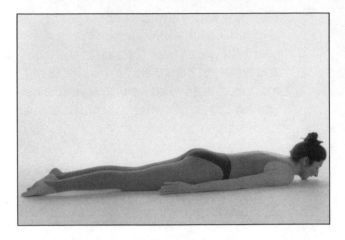

Lie on the floor face down, with arms along your sides, palms facing in towards the body. There are three arm positions that we will use in practicing this pose. Move into each variation on an inhalation, and remember to breathe as you remain in the pose. Return to the floor on an exhalation.

1 As you breathe in, imagine there are ropes attached to your fingers and someone is lifting and pulling from behind to pull your upper body away from the floor. Your arms are reaching back and your neck is long, not just the front of your neck but the back and sides of your neck as well.

Face Down Chest Openings (continued)

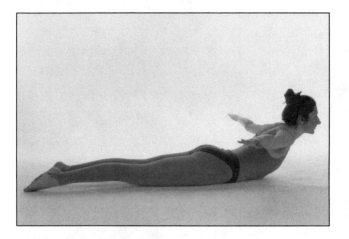 

2 Begin again from the floor, this time with your arms extended out at shoulder level. Lift your upper body away from the floor, imagining your arms as wings lifting out to the sides. Open your heart and upper chest, presenting your heart to the space in front of you. Move your shoulders away from your ears to create space around your neck. Imagine your shoulder blades sliding down your back, allowing your neck to lengthen.

3 This time, extend your arms straight over your head along the floor. Again, lift through the upper body, Superman style. This is a much harder variation, as your arms are not creating a position that will easily open your heart area. Here you will have to visualize and work towards that opening. You may find this easier if you lift your straight legs away from the floor, balancing the lift of your upper body. Experiment to see which way provides the greatest sensation of opening at the heart.

Cow Face

1 Begin in a stable pose, sitting on your legs, or cross-legged. Take one arm up and bend it at the elbow, reaching your hand behind your head down towards your back.

2 Bring the other arm down, bend at the elbow, and reach your hand up towards the other hand. The idea is not just to get the two hands together, but to also keep the spine in alignment and work towards opening the heart area. Focus on opening in the upper chest rather than allowing the lower ribs to jut out. This requires a certain amount of stretch at the armpit, and an effort to bring your elbows back rather than allowing them to collapse your shoulders forward. Keep your head tall and lifted, resisting the tendency to let it move forward.

3 Most people have difficulty getting their hands together when they first practice this pose, and we suggest the use of a belt or towel to remedy this. Hold one end of the belt in the upper hand so that it dangles down, then grab onto it with the other hand.

Pranayama—Breathing techniques

People often have the idea that breathing exercises are no big deal—after all we breathe all the time, we're just going to control it a little bit. But *pranayama* involves some very powerful techniques and it's not a good idea to begin without a certain amount of preparation. The body needs to be prepared for the stresses of the techniques. If you have been practicing the exercises presented in this workbook so far, you are already working on this. It may seem like many of these exercises are considerably more strenuous than sitting quietly and breathing, but in its own way, pranayama can be more strenuous.

Alignment

Most important in beginning pranayama is to place the body in a stable position in correct alignment in a relaxed balanced pose that takes minimal attention to maintain. This allows you to focus complete attention on the breathing practice with the least amount of tension. The best choice of positions to begin is shown in the photograph at the right, as it provides room for expansion of the lungs without distortion and tension. Fold a blanket into a shape about 3 ft. long and 8 in. wide. Position yourself on the blanket so that it supports you from the lumbar spine to the head. Fold another blanket and place it under your head, tilting your chin slightly down towards your chest. Allow your arms to fall comfortably out to your sides, somewhere between shoulder height and thigh level. When you are placing yourself in this position begin by aligning your legs symmetrically while you are sitting with the blankets just behind your buttocks. Slowly lower yourself onto the blankets, adjusting them as needed.

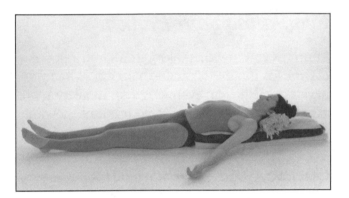

Abdominal & Thoracic Breathing

There are two major ways of deepening the breath. The first is what we often think of in relation to breathing for relaxation: as we inhale, we push the diaphragm down to create room for the filling of the lungs. This is also known as diaphragmatic breathing, or belly breathing. The other way to breathe is the thoracic breath, in which the diaphragm stays put and the ribs open and expand all around to accommodate the increased breath. The thoracic breath is an energizing breath and a more advanced technique. B.K.S. Iyengar's book, *Light on Pranayama: The Yogic Art of Breathing* published by Crossroad Publishing Company is an excellent resource.

Diaphragmatic Breathing

Breathe in through your nose, allowing your abdomen to rise as you inhale. Exhale, feeling your abdomen sink back down as the breath leaves your body. Breathe as deeply as you comfortably can, releasing your breath fully on each exhalation.

Regulating your Breath

Count as you breathe, taking the same amount of time for inhalation and exhalation. When you have established an even length of inhalation and exhalation, try lengthening your count, slowing and deepening each breath.

Corpse Pose (Savasana)

At the end of each pranayama practice, remove any blankets or pillows you used, and spend some time resting in corpse pose, breathing normally.

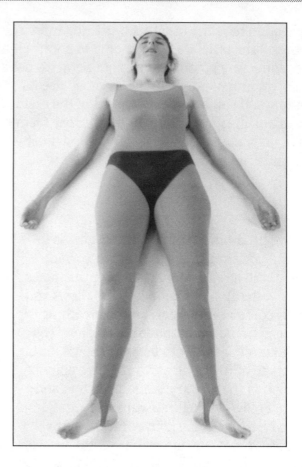

The Dance

The exercises for the fourth chakra focus on opening the area of the heart. After working with them, you will have a sense of what it feels like to physically open your body in this way. Allow your breathing to initiate your movements, with your body following the lead of the movements created by your lungs' expansion. Let this become a dance, your body's expression of the in and out of the breath, involving not just the obvious breathing movements, but going beyond them. Your breathing is the inspiration for your entire body's dance of breathing and openness at the heart.

Often the dance of the fourth chakra includes movements of giving and receiving, and the arms may be an important means of expressing this. Think of the movements of the arms and upper body that you already use to show love (for example, hugs, stroking, holding) and expand these into your dance of the heart.

Partner Work: Breathing Into the Back

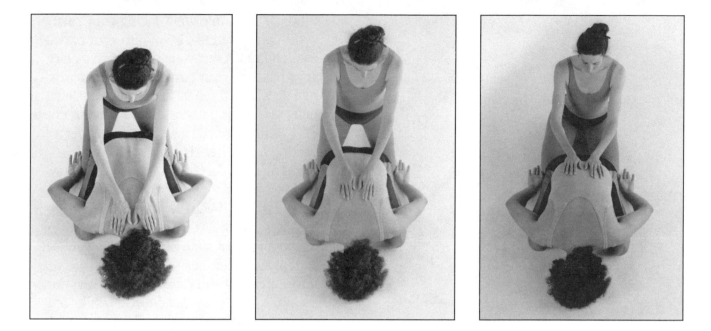

When people think about expanding their lungs while breathing, they often expand primarily to the front, opening their rib cage forward. Our lungs expand to the sides and back as well, and to practice pranayama correctly, we need to be able to do this. Working with a partner can help bring awareness and movement to the back in breathing practice. One partner takes child's pose. The other partner sits behind and places her hands gently on her partner's back, starting at the top of the back, then the middle, then the lower part of the back. In each position, the breathing partner directs his breathing towards the hands of his partner, expanding into that part of his back for a few breaths.

Partner Work: Heart Connection

Stand or sit comfortably facing your partner within arm's length. Look into your partner's eyes and reach out your right arm to place your hand on your partner's chest, approximately where the heart is. Place your left hand over your partner's hand on your chest. Feel your connection with your partner's beating heart, her rhythmic flow of life's blood moving through her body. Imagine that you are part of that circuit now, giving energy through your right hand, receiving it through your heart from her hand. Stay with this in a relaxed state for as long as you feel comfortable. Notice any tensions that creep into your body and release them with your breath. Notice your facial tension, allowing yourself to keep your face relaxed rather than forming it into a smile or trying to communicate love and compassion through your expression. Just be with yourself and be with your partner.

Partner Work: Mirrors

Stand facing your partner and imagine that you are each looking in a mirror. Each of you in turn takes the role of leader, the one looking in the mirror, while the other responds as the mirror image. This means that if the leader raises her right hand, the mirror image raises his left hand. The idea here is to practice sensitivity to each other, so the leader needs to create movement slow enough to follow—if your partner is way behind, slow down and pay attention to how they are following you, pacing yourself accordingly. When you are the following partner attempt to capture as much as you can of the person you are mirroring, including facial expressions and whatever level of subtlety is possible for you. Switch leaders to allow both partners to experience both roles.

Partner Work: Touch-point

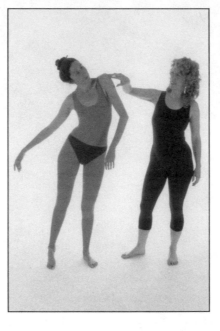

One of you stimulates movement in your partner by touching various parts of her body, while the other uses those touches as a cue to allow that part of your body to follow the touch. For example, if my partner touches my shoulder, that shoulder leads my body along until she awakens another part by touch and that part becomes the new focus.

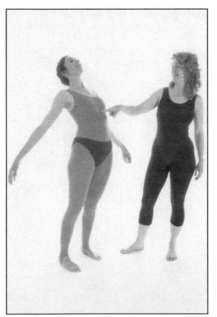

Putting It Into Practice

Giving

Give some money to a beggar on the street. Smile at a stranger who looks sad. Donate to a charitable cause. Do an afternoon of volunteer work at a hospice, a senior citizens' home, or some similar organization.

Notice when you close down, when it doesn't feel safe to give, whether it be a smile or a coin to a beggar.

Notice when you feel obligated or pressured to give at a time that it would be detrimental to yourself. How do you respond usually?

Notice where your boundaries are and what you do to enforce them or make them clear to yourself or others.

Air

Pay attention to smells, to the air and clouds and to your own breath. Practice breathing exercises at least five minutes each day; fifteen is better. When not practicing the exercises, make it a point to at least notice your breath. When does your breath get shallow, when do you take deep breaths?

Working with the element of air, try to create a feeling of lightness and expansion in your life. Don't be a heavy. Don't hang on. The heart chakra is not the place to get attached to personal ego (that was the third chakra), but is instead the place where we relinquish it. Practice relinquishing your ego in small matters where it seems like you can manage it. As you let go, a lightness will come.

Air has to do with the sense of smell, and although this sense was classically attributed to the first chakra (because animals close to the ground rely on their sense of smell more than we do), smell is more appropriately related to air and breath. Pay attention to smells, wear perfume, notice air quality, climb a mountain in the clear air, fly an airplane, make a complaint about air pollution.

Air also represents space and expansion. If we are to truly open the heart chakra, we require room to expand. We need space to ourselves, space for our feelings, space to be quiet, space to receive. This is also crucial for the work that will follow in the upper chakras that require more meditation and reflection. See what you can do to create more space for yourself.

Relationships

This is the time to work on examining and balancing your relationships. Pay attention to important relationships in your life—both the ones you like and the ones you don't like. Examine these relationships in terms of their energetic dynamics, the balance of give and take, the needs involved. What makes these relationships important to you? What needs to be improved?

Take extra time for your positive relationships during this period. Hire a babysitter or take time off work and go away with your spouse for the weekend. Have a small dinner party to reconnect with old friends. Take extra time for your children, improving your relationship with them, really paying attention to the patterns of interaction between you. Make a call or a visit to an aging parent or relative. Make amends to someone you may have hurt in a relationship.

Make a point to relate to everyone you come in contact with, even if only for a brief moment. Say "Hello" to the checker at the grocery store, ask how her day is going. Take time to meet the eyes of your bank teller or waitress in a restaurant.

If you are forced by circumstance to relate to someone you dislike, through a job or housing situation, notice your internal responses to the qualities you dislike in them (see *Rejected selves* exercise, opposite). Ask yourself what there might be for you to learn from this person or situation. Make it a point to do one thing each day to improve the relationship, either by talking with the person about what you don't like or by making offerings of good will in their direction.

Examine your relationships to food, substances, work, nature, or study. What binds you to unhealthy practices or separates you from the healthy relationship you would like to have? Take steps to improve these relationships by honoring the underlying needs in a healthier way.

Journal Exercises

1. Love

Who do you love?

Make a list of people that you love or have loved strongly in your life. What are their common characteristics? How does thinking about them make you feel?

2. Self-acceptance

Make a list of all the faults that you berate yourself for having, all the judgments you have of yourself. List all the ways that you do not fulfill your expectations of how you "should" be. Go through the list again, examining the origins of each item on your list, including where you got the idea that each trait is negative. Decide for yourself whether each trait is truly something that is negative, or whether it is merely something that others did not approve of. Your ideas about these traits, as well as the traits themselves, have come from childhood experiences, cultural conditioning, situational circumstances, or survival strategies. Feel the predicament that created each, the forces that you were responding to. Go through your list and forgive yourself for each of them. This doesn't mean you necessarily accept the trait—just that you forgive yourself for having it.

Next make a list of what you might need in order to be able to change some of these traits. For instance, to change being sloppy, you might need to slow down a little, and make more time for yourself. To be less irritable you might need to learn to ask for what you want in a direct way.

3. Rejected selves

This fits in with the journal exercise described above, but goes a little deeper. A rejected self is an aspect of personality that we had to overcome in order to survive—something we had to reject. For some people, anger is a rejected self. For others it might be laziness, shyness or even boldness. The key to recognizing a rejected self is our tendency to judge others for having this trait, and continually manifesting friends or co-workers that have extreme levels of the trait. Thus someone who is a workaholic will have a rejected self that is lazy, and will have a tendency to harshly judge others who are lazy and/or manifest a mate or coworker who glorifies in kicking back and taking it easy. Those who have rejected selves of anger will often find themselves in relationship with people who have a temper.

Journal Exercises

Reclaiming a rejected self does not mean that you necessarily embody that negative trait. It means that you accept the part of you that might long to have a little more of that quality. The workaholic might see that she'd like to slow down, the sweet and docile housewife may realize she does not always stand up for herself, and could benefit from the anger she's rejected.

Reclaiming a rejected self helps us become more balanced within ourselves, less judgmental of others, and less apt to wind up with the epitome of our worst fears sitting across from us at the breakfast table or the office desk. Once we accept it in ourselves, we need not manifest it in others.

Make a list of traits that you find objectionable in others, starring the ones that especially push your buttons. Put an extra check mark next to the ones that have been common in your friends, lovers, or coworkers, or have been recurrent issues in your life.

• What was your own programming around these traits?

• What would have happened to you in your family if you had indulged in this behavior?

• What price do you pay now for being unable to have this behavior available to you?

• What part of yourself do you continually engage to keep your rejected self suppressed (such as an inner critic, a slave driver, a doubter, etc.)?

• What would happen if that inner control relaxed and you developed a bit of this trait?

• What could you do differently to allow this part of you to appear now and then?

4. Mirror exercise

This is simple, yet profound. Look into a mirror, reach your hands toward it, and say "I love you." What happens when you attempt this? What inner voices do you hear? Can you do it in front of someone else? Does it feel true?

Journal Exercises

5. Balance

Achieving balance within ourselves is the first step toward achieving balance with others. Below is a list of opposites with a line indicating that they exist on a continuum. Copy this list and make an "X" on the line at the point that most accurately describes you on this continuum.

Passive————————————————————————————Aggressive
Feminine————————————————————————————Masculine
Receiving————————————————————————————Giving
Inner-directed————————————————————————Outer-directed
Mental activity————————————————————————Physical activity
Private————————————————————————————Public
Introverted————————————————————————Extroverted
Ordered————————————————————————————Chaotic
Positive attitude————————————————————Negative attitude
Left brained (logical)————————————————Right brained (creative)
Being————————————————————————————Doing
Reason————————————————————————————Intuition
Quiet————————————————————————————Active
Success————————————————————————————Failure
Transcendence————————————————————Immanence
Resistant————————————————————————Yielding
Happy————————————————————————————Sad

How close does your line of X's come to the middle? What are some of the consistent imbalances? What are the causes for these and what can be done to help bring them into greater balance?

6. Reassessment

• What have you learned about yourself as you've worked through the fourth chakra activities?

• What areas of this chakra do you need to work on? How will you do that?

• What areas of this chakra do you feel pleased with? How can you utilize these strengths?

Entering Sacred Space

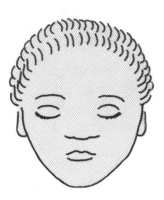

Healing Meditation

Healing is an integral part of the heart chakra. Healing channels come from the heart and flow down the inside of the arms, down the yin meridians that connect with the heart, lungs, and pericardium, and out through the hands. Close your eyes, focus on your heart and deepen your breathing. Imagine a green light flooding your heart with a strong healing vibration, coming in from everywhere around you until it is so full it flows over and into your body, down your arms and into your hands until your hands are so full they are spilling over.

When you feel the healing energy running most strongly, imagine an aspect of yourself or a friend (with their permission) who would like to receive this energy. Imagine the green light spilling over from you into them and pouring into whatever place they most need healing until it too is filling to abundance. Allow this to continue as long as it is comfortable and you remain centered within yourself. Then let the energy slowly subside. Reestablish your own boundaries, and ground yourself (as described in the first chakra) to drain off any excess charge you may have retained. If you feel depleted, imagine that green light entering your head from your crown and your feet.

You might want to do this meditation prior to giving a massage and let the energy flow through your hands as you connect with another.

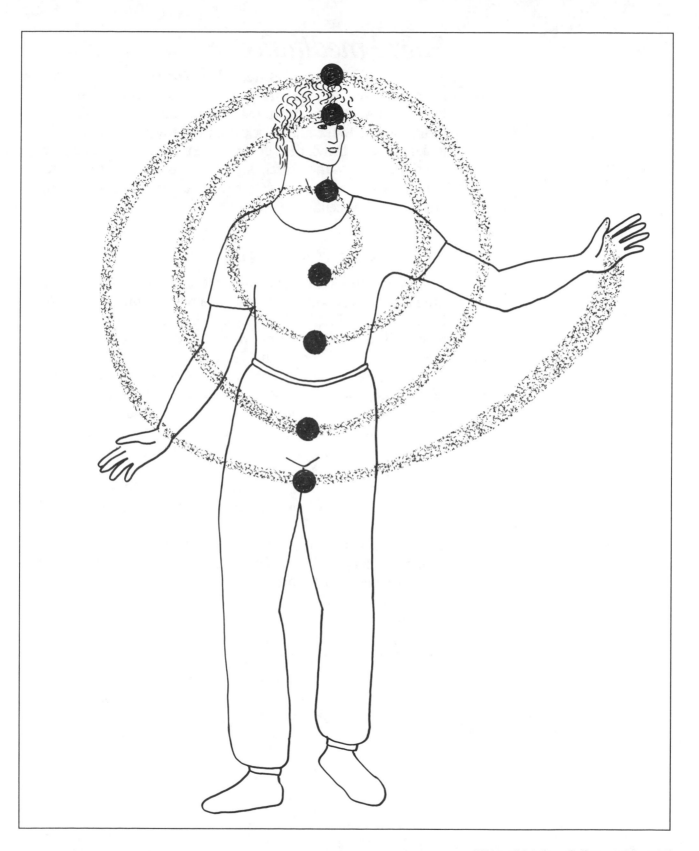

Spiral meditation

Examine the spiral energy pattern shown on the previous page. Sit quietly in meditation and imagine the spiral energy in your own body, beginning at the heart. Let it swoop down to the third chakra and up to the fifth (clockwise from the perspective of looking at your belly), then down to the second chakra and up to the sixth, down to the first chakra and up to the seventh and out. Repeat the process in reverse order, channeling energy from the outside into the center of your heart.

Appreciation Ritual

If you and your lover are at a tough place in your relationship, this little ritual can do wonders to restore a sense of love and being loved. It does not replace working out difficulties, but certainly helps build a foundation upon which to work them out in an atmosphere of love and mutual respect.

Sit opposite your partner on the floor or in chairs of similar height. Take a moment to look into each other's eyes in silence. Think about what you like or love about this person.

Then begin to tell each other about the traits you appreciate, taking turns, making one statement each, and continuing until you run out of things to say, or the energy changes. You can talk about qualities or actions, such as "I appreciate the way you re-member to call me when you're going to be late." Do not omit the little things.

The only rule for this ritual is that no criticism or conditionalizing is allowed. Don't say, "I appreciate your cooking, but I wish you'd do it more." Simply, "I appreciate your cooking," is enough.

This ritual can also be used in group situations. One member of the group at a time gets in the middle, and each of the others takes a turn complimenting that person.

Self Blessing Ritual

This is similar to the appreciation ritual, but you don't need anyone else to do it with you. Take some water, perfume, fragrant oil, or other substance that feels special to you with which you can anoint yourself.

Take a preparatory bath, and find a time and place where you can be naked and private. You may wish to to do this in front of a mirror, or you may not.

Take a bit of the liquid you are using and touch it to your feet. Say aloud something like:

"Blessed be my feet that carry me along my path. I thank them for taking me on this journey."

Next come up to your knees, and say:

"Blessed be my knees that bend so I may walk. May I be both flexible and strong in all my actions."

Continue on to your groin, and say:

"Blessed be my genitals that give me pleasure. May they be both protected and pleased."

Continue on to your belly, your breasts (male or female), your throat, your mouth, your eyes, etc. Include any other part you feel you want to bless. You may also wish to bless each of your chakras, for the role they play in your life. The statements above are just examples. Your statements will, of course, be your own blessings as they come spontaneously to you.

This ritual may also be done with someone you are close to, each of you taking a turn blessing the other.

Group Ritual
Materials Needed

Feathers
Music

Breathing & Grounding

Take hands in a circle. Close your eyes and tune into your own individual bodies, feeling your weight, gravity pulling you deep into the ground, into roots that go deep into the earth. Spend as much time as needed here, one person (or more) guiding the visualization so that all the participants have the same imagery to work with as they ground. Breathing deeply and easily, bring awareness into each part of your body, until you feel life energy flowing through you.

Passing Breath Around Circle

One person feels the energy that is flowing through them concentrate in their breath as they take a deep breath in, then they blow that energy out through their mouth toward the body of the person on their left, who breathes it in and then passes it on in the same way. Send the breath around the circle three times, slow the first time, then speeding up. In this way the circle is cast with breath, the element of the heart chakra.

Moving Through First Three Chakras

This part may be done formally by choosing one or two of the movements from each of the first three chakras and having one person (or perhaps one person for each chakra) lead the group through the movements, visualizing the energy moving up through each chakra. If you are working by yourself, allow those images to flow through your mind as you move. A less formal approach would be to improvise the movements for each chakra as the visualization verbalizes attributes or qualities of each. The more familiar you are with the movements of each chakra—the more you've practiced—the easier this informal approach will be. Either way, finish at the heart.

Bringing in the Upper Three Chakras

Imagine reaching up, way beyond the top of your body, way beyond the physical boundaries of your skin, out into the universe, out into the place that is larger than you as an individual. Reach for the energy of spirit and pull it down into you through the top of your head, the crown chakra, down through your third eye, down through your throat, and into your heart, where it mingles with the energy of earth that has traveled up from your roots through your lower chakras and into your heart.

Moving from the Breath

From that focus at the heart, begin to pay attention to your breath and the movements that naturally occur as your lungs expand and release. Allow your body to emphasize those movements, to make the movements larger and spread them into the surrounding areas of your body. For example, as you breathe in, your chest expands and this may lift your head up gently and begin to tilt it back or to the side. As you breathe out, your head may curve gently down and around as the movement focus travels to the belly and pelvis, perhaps shifting the hips and twisting the torso. As the breath enters again it may expand into one arm which lifts through the air, moving through space. You may pick up feathers (the soft type, like peacock feathers) and expand your movements out towards other participants, touching them softly with the soft airiness of the feather, which provides another stimulation to motivate your partner's movement in addition to their breath motions.

> Music: *Lullaby for the Hearts of Space*
> (use this for the next section as well).

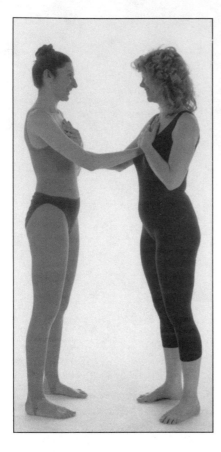

Heart touches

Choose a partner. Follow the instructions for the Heart Connection on page 176. If this feels too close for comfort, position your hands in a more symbolic way over each other's heart, and share that center through the image of touching heartbeats, rather than the physical sensation. This can be done with eyes closed, or with eyes gazing at each other.

If there is time, you may finish with this partner and move to another, experiencing a heart connection with several people before moving to the circle of hearts.

Circle of hearts

Form a circle, each participant facing to your left and placing your left hand on the heart of the person whose back you are facing. Sing together, as you stand in a circle connected through the heart. (See music opposite.)

Sharing—What do you love?

Allow your hands to come away from hearts and rest easily around each other or hold hands as you face into the circle. Go around the circle as many times as there is energy for, sharing images of what you love. This can be people, places, things, interactions, ideas, whatever comes to mind from your heart.

Group hug to ground

The group may be hugging already, but give that your attention, looking around at these people you've shared your heart with. Then bring the energy down to the ground, with a sound if you like.

I am a Circle

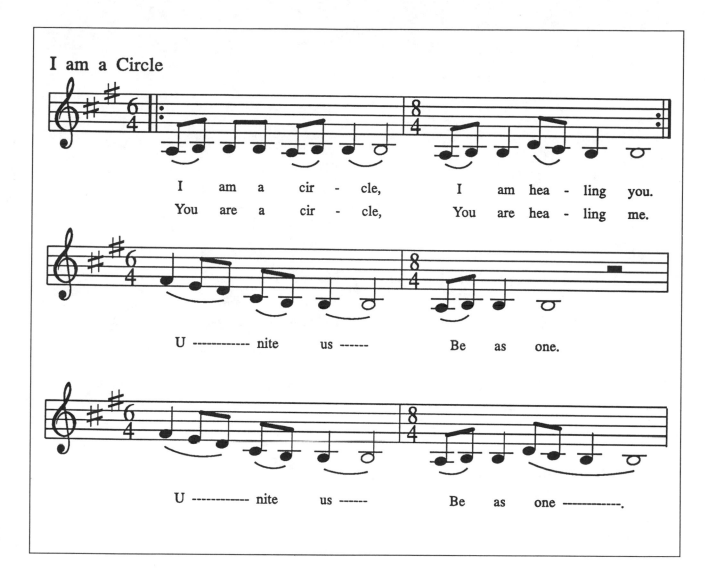

I am a cir - cle, I am hea - ling you.
You are a cir - cle, You are hea - ling me.

U ----------- nite us ------ Be as one.

U ----------- nite us ------ Be as one ------------.

Resources

Books

Hendrix, Harville. *Getting the Love You Want.* Harper & Row.

Iyengar, B.K.S. *Light on Pranayama: The Yogic Art of Breathing.* Crossroad Publishing Company.

Johnson, Sonia. *The Ship that Sailed into the Living Room.* Wildfire Press.

Malone, Thomas Patrick. *The Art of Intimacy.* Prentice Hall

Ram Dass & Gorman, Paul. *How Can I Help? Stories & Reflections on Service.* Knopf.

Rama, Swami, Ballentine, Rudolph, & Hymes, Alan. *Science of Breath: A Practical Guide.* Himalayan International Institute.

Shandler, Michael & Nina. *Ways of Being Together.* Schocken.

Welwood, John. *Challenge of the Heart.* Shambhala.

Music

Braheny, Kevin. *Lullaby from the Hearts of Space.*

Halpern, Steven. *Spectrum Suite.* (and many others)

Ojas. *Lotusongs II.*

Roach, Steve. *Structures from Silence.*

Chakra Five
Sound

Getting Started

Where Are You Now?

Write down your thoughts or feelings about the following concepts that relate to the fifth chakra:

Vibration	*Communication*
Rhythm	*Creativity*
Sound	*Singing/Chanting*
Harmony	*Writing*
Connection	*Public Speaking*
Telepathy	

This chakra involves the neck, throat, mouth and jaw. How do you feel about these areas of your body? Are there any difficulties you've had in these areas at any time during your life?

Altar Arrangement

Our main color in this chakra is a bright turquoise blue, so candles and altar cloths and other symbols should be chosen accordingly. This is the chakra for communication and creativity, so there are no limits to how you may want to symbolize this. You have set up several altars by now; let your creativity flourish.

If there is someone you wish to communicate with or are having difficulty with, place a picture of that person on your altar and speak to it everyday. If you don't have a picture, use some other item that reminds you of them.

Words are part of communication. Simply writing a clear affirmation or a statement of a particular intent on a three by five card can serve as a reminder of that intent whenever you look at your altar. You may wish to read it aloud whenever you see it, and the mere act of writing it concisely requires you to focus on its essential aspects.

Other objects to put on the altar are musical instruments or soundmakers—bells, singing bowls, rattles, chimes.

Correspondences

Sanskrit name	Visuddha
Meaning	Purification
Location	Throat
Element	Ether, sound
Main Issue	Communication
Goals	Self-expression, harmony with others, creativity, good communication, resonance with self and others
Malfunction	Inability to express or release, blocked creativity, sore throats, stiff shoulders, tight necks
Color	Bright blue
Planet	Mercury
Foods	Fruit
Right	To Speak
Stones	Turquoise
Animals	Elephant, bull
Operating principle	Sympathetic Vibration
Yoga Path	Mantra yoga
Archetype	Hermes, Sarasvati the Messenger

Sharing the Experience

"I burned my communication candle a lot and thought things at it that I wanted to communicate and finally got a chance to say all those things to the people I was thinking them at, and that helped a lot. It also helped ease some of the pressure I had been feeling over my heart, because a lot of the things were heart related. I also started voice lessons this month, and that is helping me open my throat chakra. I have been practicing a lot, and it even seems to be changing my speaking voice."

•

"My communications this month were mostly centered around getting flyers out and communicating with people about this event that I am working on. Other than that I had a big blow up with my boyfriend which needs to be worked out. But it opened up communication."

•

"I have to communicate all day long at my job, talking to people about energy conservation. I feel good, like I'm doing this little piece of saving the planet. My husband finally is back from overseas and it takes a lot of communicating to adjust to him being back in the family again."

"I wrote a lot of letters to people overseas, unfinished stuff that I hadn't said. And, with people that I was intimidated by, higher than me, jobwise or whatever. Normally I'd keep my mouth shut, but I opened my mouth and nothing bad happened because of it, so... I have a lot to work on with this one. Oh, one thing that's been happening is that a few times, when people aren't really saying things to me, they're just thinking something, I have fully answered their question like they've been talking to me. And I don't even know it's happening until they tell me they were only thinking that, but I hear it loud and clear like they were talking. I suppose my telepathy channel is opening from the kundalini energy I have been running."

•

"I feel like I've done some great communicating this month. I was able to communicate with my husband about the divorce settlement in a clear way. It feels like we're getting to a place beyond fighting. My communication with a lot of people, my kids for instance, is much clearer as far as boundaries go. I have been able to be more spontaneous with communication, something that's always been hard for me."

"This has been a month of communication for me also. I've traveled with work and done a lot of trade shows and conducted a lot of business. This is probably the first month that I seriously got into doing the physical exercises. Last year I was in a collision and I have been fighting a whiplash condition and I've been receiving chiropractic treatments. Last week, when I went in for an adjustment, some things had opened up, so I'm seeing the results of my work. That was great, because there's been a lot of physical discomfort. I also have had a terrible wariness of doing a journal, of writing anything on paper. After class last time, I bought a journal, and have taken it with me on my travels. On the last trip I finally started writing and it's just flowing."

●

"I also had a fight with my boyfriend. But I did something else that was even bigger—I wrote a letter to my real father. I've never told him how I felt about what's happened in the past, where I was the result of a divorce and he was never a part of my life at all, and I mailed that and that was hard but felt good. He called me this morning and we talked, and told me he was really sorry. He says he wants to write and keep in touch. No matter what comes of it, I feel better just being heard."

Understanding the Concept

As we leave the balance point of chakra four, we use our will to push our breath upwards, into our throat chakra, where we turn it into *sound, communication,* and *creativity*. Here we enter the bright blue of the fifth chakra, whose Sanskrit name, *Visuddha,* means "purification." Our lotus at this level has sixteen petals, upon which are written all the vowels of the Sanskrit language. The vowel sounds comprise the energy of spirit, while the consonants, which appear on the petals of all the lower chakras, shape spirit into the material world. As we enter the more etheric dimensions of the upper chakras, we enter the realm of spirit that pervades all matter. Communication is a link, capable of describing both spirit and matter.

Sound

The associated element of this chakra is *sound*. Hindus believe that the whole universe came into being through sound. In Hindu mythology, it is believed that at the end of time, Mother Kali, the destroyer aspect of the Goddess, will come and remove the letters from the petals of the chakras, thus removing all sound and collapsing the universe once again into its original void. It is through sound and communication that we continually create and breathe spirit into our world, keeping it alive and vital. Sound gives the spirit form. For this reason, sound and communication are connected to creativity, our unique expression of spirit.

Purification

Visuddha as purification has a dual meaning in the throat chakra. The refinement of our physical vibrations, necessary for penetration into the higher levels, requires a certain amount of bodily purification through attention to diet, substance intake, activities, and meditation techniques. Through this process of purification, we attune to subtler levels of perception, aurally, visually, and psychically, and thus are able to receive more information with which to expand our consciousness.

Sound also creates purification through its ordering effect on both matter and consciousness. To purify something is to return it to its essential nature, to bring it into its natural order—that which emanates from its center. Sound, running through the head of a drum with sand on it, will dance the sand into an ordered mandala-like pattern—a pattern that radiates from a center. Communication can order our world, whether we are asking for a change in our lives, or simply sharing our perception of order with another. Likewise, chanting of tones can have an ordering and purifying effect on our own center, physically and mentally. Thus as a meditation technique, the use of rhythms, chants and tones helps us to center and "purify" our focus.

Vibration

Sound is the rhythmic vibration of air molecules. As we enter the fifth chakra realm of sound and communication, we experience the world in terms of vibration, the operating principle of the fifth chakra. Matter, movement, and energy, from our first three chakras, have now entered into a pattern of stable interrelationship (chakra four). As we incorporate the next level, we experience these interrelationships as vibration. It's like opening the hood of our car while the engine is idling; even though we know combustion is moving pistons in cylinders thousands of times per minute, we can only experience the *vibration* of the engine when we pay attention to it. We don't see or hear the minute interactions, only a hum that lets us know whether the engine is well-tuned. Likewise, when we meet a person, or experience an event, our consciousness cannot perceive every minute internal process within the person or event—we experience instead the overall vibrational quality.

This is the perceptual framework of the fifth chakra—sound and vibration. The work of the fifth chakra involves fine-tuning our own vibrational energies for clearer self-expression, better communication with others, and general harmony with our environment.

Rhythm Entrainment

All vibration is a rhythmic oscillation through time, and the pattern of that rhythm is what constitutes communication. All life is rhythmic, from the beating of one's heart, to the diurnal cycle of days and nights, to the vibration of brain waves and nerve impulses. When these vibrations enter into a state of harmony amongst themselves, there is a profound sense of connectedness, deepening, and expansion that we can experience. This occurs in the following way:

All rhythm is subject to a principle called *resonance*, also known as *sympathetic vibration* or *rhythm entrainment*. Resonance results when rhythms or wave forms of similar frequency (vibrations per unit of time) enter into phase with each other, in other words, lock into the same rhythm. Thus the ticks and tocks of the grandfather clocks in the antique shop all occur simultaneously, and women who live together will often menstruate at the same time of the month. Two people rhythmically entrained in their conversation may blurt out the same phrase in unison, and a drummer locked into phase with the rhythm of music enters into an ecstatic state of unity with the music, making it difficult to miss a beat.

When two wave forms enter into phase with each other, their amplitude is increased (see diagram at right). This is called constructive interference. We can think of amplitude as that which gives us volume or intensity. Therefore, when we are in resonance with something—be it a piece of music, conversation with another person, or a basic truth we are hearing for the first time—the intensity of our experience is increased. There is an expansive feeling that reaches outward and back in again, all in a harmonic rhythm that entrains body, mind and spirit to a central unifying pulse. To be unified within and expanded without is to combine the transcendence of the upper chakras and the immanence of the lower chakras into a single experience.

Wave forms that are in phase with each other tend to remain in phase, as if knitted together by the power of the entrainment. When we are in resonance with another person, we want to stay with that person and it can be painful to be ripped away. A piece of music we especially like resonates in our mind long after it has stopped playing. (Advertising jingles are designed to resonate with basic human frequencies for just this reason.) We might think of sleep as a process whereby our thoughts, breathing patterns, heart rate, and rhythmic body pulses enter into resonance with each

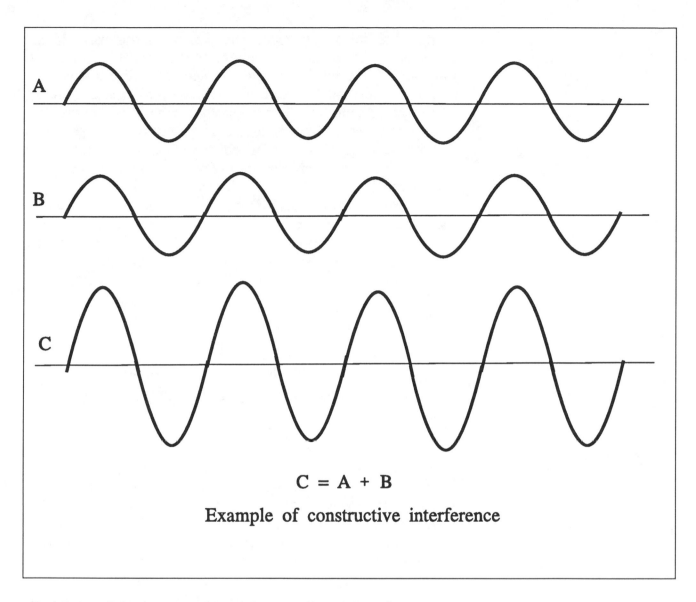

$$C = A + B$$

Example of constructive interference

other. It is a disharmonious sound that usually wakes us from slumber, and there is usually a strong urge to return to that deep harmonious state—unless we have a strong resonance with what we are going to do that day!

Even when an instrument is quiet it has the properties of being "tuned" to a particular frequency. Through contact with a similar frequency the resting object may be "awakened." Thus if we both have violins tuned to each other, I can get a resting string to vibrate on your violin simply by playing that same note on my own. If we apply this principle to consciousness, then it follows that we can activate a state of consciousness in someone else through the expression of our own vibrations if there is a basic vibrational similarity to begin with. Evidence of this principle can be seen in cases of telepathic communication, vibrational healing, awakening of Kundalini energies from contact with a master, or the power of music to inspire profound states of consciousness. During rock concerts, where the beat is strong and there are large numbers of people listening to the same rhythms, many people have experienced an entrainment of consciousness. Some people experience this as an exciting state of consciousness or even a group mind.

We've all experienced the way someone can only understand what they are ready to hear. On a grander scale, paradigm shifts in mass consciousness occur when enough of a population (critical mass) upholds certain ideals and thus awakens the rest of the population.

Communication

Communication itself is a rhythmic activity. Studies have shown that listeners and speakers enter into entrainment as they converse and that the depth of understanding from that communication relates to one's ability to enter into that resonance. The more we enter into resonance with our internal rhythms the more easily we can strike up resonance with another and have clear and profound communication. Next time you are struggling with difficult communication, pay attention to the rhythms of speech between you and your partner and see if you can develop a resonance to help the communication process. Even chanting together for a few minutes before conversing can greatly enhance the flow of communication that follows.

Through harmonious communication, we enhance and expand the spirit within. We can transcend physical limitations of time and space—a phone call can reach across great distance, a letter or recorded message preserves communication through time. As we move from the lower chakras to the upper, our pattern is one of expansion and transcendence. At the level of chakra five, we begin to work with the world in symbols, as through words we represent the physical world and find a way to reach beyond its limitations.

Chanting

Chanting is a way of harmonizing our own vibrations through the conscious use of sound. It can also be used as a group activity to enhance resonance and communication with the group as a whole, and becomes a powerful tool for generating a cohesive collective consciousness. Group singing and chanting are traditional shamanic techniques for creating a healing vibration, group mind, or access to the spirit world through altered states of consciousness.

Creativity

As a channel for our expression, the fifth chakra is, in its highest form, associated with creativity. All creativity is a form of communication. Through communication we create our lives and circumstances. The arts, in whatever form, are a complex form of communication. While working on this chakra, allow yourself to enter into a childlike state of creativity, working with voice, writing, color, dance or whatever form of expression appeals to you.

Excess and Deficiency

If the fifth chakra is energetically excessive, a person might talk a lot without saying very much. It's as if the mouth needs to keep busy, but the words are not engaged with the body or the deeper parts of our spirit. We store stress as a "charge" in the body, experienced as tension. The fifth chakra, along with the hands and feet, is one of the primary places in the body where we can discharge energy and release tension. If we are overly charged, there may be a tendency to discharge through the throat chakra, through constant talking or even yelling. Allowing yourself to discharge consciously, by releasing loud sounds from deep within the body in a context that is not harmful, can release tension and allow the fifth chakra to open and function normally.

If the chakra is deficient in energy there is difficulty in communication. Tight throats, knotted shoulders, and a voice without rhythm or resonance indicate fifth chakra blockage. This can be due to poor self esteem, family patterns that discouraged communication ("Don't talk, don't trust, don't feel"), or simply poor grounding, which offers too little support for the will, the breath, and the voice.

Opening the fifth chakra requires bodily purification, the daily practice of using the voice, and attention to the rhythms of our life and our communication patterns. The result is more powerful communication, profound states of consciousness, and greater creativity.

Working with Movement & Sound

Neck Rolls

This is a somewhat controversial topic, as many chiropractors and other specialists in spinal work feel that it is unwise to roll the head around on the spinal axis. Because of this, it is important to take care in this exercise to keep the neck long and not to allow the weight of the head to "crunch" down as you circle. Start by lifting the head as if there was a rope attached to the crown, pulling the weight of your head up and out of the top of the spine. Continuing to feel this length, allow your head to fall forward, keeping the spine in place so that the back of the neck stretches. Slowly shift the position of your head so that the stretch travels to the side of your neck. Think of that rope pulling the head away from the top of the spine as you reach the head towards the back, not allowing the head to drop down, but rather experiencing it as reaching back, stretching the front of the neck. Carefully continue the circle, moving your head to the other side and then back to the front. If this creates any discomfort, stretch your neck by allowing the weight of your head to fall forward, back, and to each side in turn, stretching in each position but returning to center before going to the next position rather than circling around.

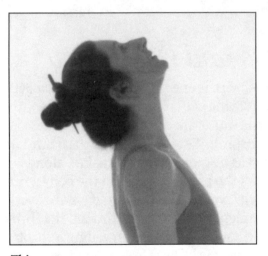

This

Not This

Shoulder Rolls

Circle your shoulders one at a time, forward and back, then both at the same time. This may feel unrelated to the throat area, but freeing the tension held in your shoulders allows considerably more freedom in the area of the throat chakra.

Fish

Align your body lying down on your back with your legs extended in line with your hip joints. Place your arms so that your hands rest palm down. As you inhale, arch your back lifting your chest and the front of your neck. Allow your head to fall backwards, resting the top of your head lightly on the floor. Use the strength of your arms to assist your back in holding this position—do not let your head take the weight of your upper body. Pull your shoulders away from your ears, lengthening your neck and being aware of the opening there. Continue breathing. To come down, uncurl your spine from the bottom up to your head, gently lowering your back and head to the floor.

Vocal warm-ups

Begin by opening your mouth as wide as you can, stretching it open, forcing a yawn if you can. Feel the openness and allow sounds to come out as you stretch it, twist it, move it all around, wiggling, mashing and squishing all the muscles around the mouth and jaw and lower part of the face. We ordinarily have a narrow range of motion in this area, and this is an opportunity to exercise all the muscles that we use to speak, trying out positions and configurations that perhaps would feel silly in another context. Work not just with the lips and jaw, but with the inside of the mouth as well, the tongue and the inside of the lips, sucking, pushing, clicking, making strange sounds with your mouth. This will loosen up the physical apparatus that we use to create sound, allowing more freedom and less strain in your vocalizations.

Chakra Vowel Sounds

Take a deep breath and intone the vowel sounds of each chakra in turn. Try to feel the chakra vibrate as you make its tone. Sing loudly and fully.

1 o as in rope

2 oo as in due

3 ah as in father

4 ay as in play

5 ee as in see

6 mmm, nnn

7 ngngng as in sing

Group Sounding Meditation

This exercise is adapted from Emily Conrad Da'oud, a prominent teacher in the field of movement meditation. Each participant sits in alignment, either in a circle or wherever in the room each chooses. During the time allotted (at least 10 minutes, a half hour or more is better) each participant has four choices of what they can be doing:

1. back of throat hum: hum with mouth closed throughout the exhalation

2. staccato breaks in breath: humming as in 1, but stopping the hum and the exhalation at intervals of your choosing (anything from fast bursts to long hums with just one or two breaks—or any combination)

3. lip beats in breath to form "ma-ma-mo-mo-me-me-ma"

4. silence, being present in your body, in this room, open to the sounding that is going on around you (or the silence)

This is an exercise in experiencing the creation, sensation, and reception of sound. Drop your expectations and goals and be present, participating in the creation of this sound environment.

Moving to Music

Experiment with a variety of music styles, allowing your movement to express the different ways your body responds to each style. Don't worry about "dancing" in a preconceived way, just allow your body to respond to the sounds and rhythms. Try music from other cultures and other parts of the world, as well as the variety of music styles available within your own culture.

The Dance

The dance of the fifth chakra is a throat dance that opens and moves energy through and around the throat, mouth, shoulders, creating sound spontaneously as you move. See where the sounds take you in movement, play with the rhythms of your sounds and steps.

Putting It Into Practice

Purification

The name Visuddha means purification. This can be interpreted in two ways: One is that we need to purify our bodies to refine our overall physical vibrations enough to access the higher chakras above. As the gateway between mind and body, the throat chakra refines the gross vibrations of physicality into the subtle vibrations of light and thought. This is not to say that the higher chakras are better than the more physical lower chakras, just that their natures are different.

Throat chakra problems on the physical plane, such as sore throats or tight necks and shoulders, can be exacerbated by the use of substances, including everything from alcohol or tobacco to food additives. Clearing ourselves of these substances can help loosen our neck and shoulders, clear our throats and contribute to the healing of sore throats and related illnesses. Complete healing, however, is usually a more complex matter.

Work on the fifth chakra includes a certain amount of purification, such as a program of abstinence from any harmful chemicals you might habitually ingest, or the temporary restriction of certain foods.

Toning

Sound can order and purify one's state of consciousness. As described earlier, sound has the ability to organize fine bits of matter, such as grains of salt or sand, liquid, or smoke, into intricate mandala-like patterns. Coherent, rhythmic sound can create a resonance with our thoughts, breathing, heart rate, and brain waves. This is the principle behind mantras.

It also follows that we can develop the habit of purifying our own sacred space with the use of sound through chanting or toning. A mantra classically used for this purpose is Om Ah Hum, but a series of good long *Oms* works equally well.

This should be done in a centered, focused way, preferably sitting with spine aligned, and with no interruptions. Begin by going inside, paying attention to your breath, and listening to the sounds around you. Then, slowly and quietly at first, allow a sound to emerge from your throat—any syllable or pitch that feels right. Open your throat, your breath and your heart, and let the sound come out as fully as possible. After you get the sound going, temper it with listening to get a clear sound, one that reverberates through you. It is important to try different pitches—every person's body is different and resonates to different pitches. You might also try this with the seed sounds or vowel sounds of each chakra.

The longer you sing, the clearer your singing will become (up to a point; don't sing yourself hoarse, or you can hurt your vocal chords). There is no magic formula for how long to chant in order to have the sense of purifying the space. Many people sing two or three Oms and expect to feel a change, but it usually takes much more than that. For stronger effects, try chanting 30 minutes or more. Otherwise, chant until you feel a sense of inner clarity and calm. Then notice how your activities proceed afterward. Is your meditation or communication with another more effective? Does your body feel different?

Rhythm

Paying attention to rhythm and how it affects us is the tuning of the fifth chakra. Look at your life in terms of its rhythms—your work, your play, your sexuality, your productivity. Get a biorhythm chart done and see if it has any correlation to your life. (Biorhythm charts make predictions on your "highs" and "lows" of three aspects: your emotional, physical, and mental cycles.)

Make a chart of your cycles of high and low energy. Look at your eating and sleeping cycles and compare. Looking at cycles in your life over the years, seeing the periods of activity and periods of retreat, can broaden your understanding of where you are now.

For women, the menstrual cycle is a natural rhythm worth paying attention to. Many cultures have built in specific activities in response to women's cycles, but you can take this opportunity to find what works for you—when do you seem to want to go inwards and meditate? At what point in the cycle are your sexual drives stimulated most easily? What other correlations can you notice and respond to in organizing your life?

Pay attention to rhythm when you are walking, dancing, talking, cooking, or making love. Allow yourself to surrender to the experience of being rhythmically entrained in whatever activity you are doing.

Singing

Singing is a throat chakra activity, so give yourself permission to sing as much as you can while you are working on this chakra. If you feel you don't sing well, and don't want to sing with others around, you can sing in your car, sing in the shower, or sing along with records you like. The idea is to open your voice and get some energy reverberating through the fifth chakra. Taking a few singing lessons can do a lot to help open the throat chakra as well.

Chanting and Drumming

The use of chanting for purification described above is the use of single pure tones. Another kind of chanting that gives a different effect is the repetition of rhythm sounds, phrases, or music in conjunction with drumming. Here the tone is less important than the rhythm. This has long been a Shamanic technique to obtain access to altered states of consciousness. It can be done alone or with a group, but generally the effect is more powerful with a group.

Try this on your own by getting a drum (and, believe it or not, the bottom of a five-gallon plastic container can work if you don't have a drum) and beating out a rhythm for yourself. Allow yourself to let go into the rhythm, to enter into a trance state induced by the rhythm. This can also be done by letting someone else drum for you, allowing you to go deeper into the trance state. Notice what you feel like before and after. (Tapes of Shamanic drumming rhythms are also available at most Metaphysical book stores.)

Listening and Taking In

The other side of communication is listening. Nurture your fifth chakra with silence, taking in sounds from the outside. Practice silence for a given period—a day, a few hours, at a meeting, or when someone is talking to you.

Listen to music, experiencing a variety of styles and notice how they affect you. Go to a concert and take in the sounds around you.

Read a book. Pay attention to the rhythm of the words you are reading as well as the content. This is especially powerful with poetry.

Active Listening

Active listening is a communication skill that helps people feel they are being heard. The principle is very simple. One person sits quietly and listens while the other person speaks without interruption about something that is bothering them, or whatever it is they want to say. When they are through, the person listening simply repeats back to them what they heard, without interpretation, judgment, argument, or comment, regardless of whether the listener agrees or disagrees. A listener might answer with a statement like, "What I hear you saying is that you feel tired of being the one who always has to initiate sexual contact, and that it makes you feel like you are not attractive to me. Is that correct?" The listener can then check to see if they understood the speaker correctly, and if so can then proceed to tell their side of the story in a similar fashion, with the first person responding with an active listening statement. This technique can do wonders to help solve communication difficulties.

Creativity

Enhance your writing, singing, music playing, dance, drama, painting, or simply living your life, with greater creativity. Whatever you're doing, allow yourself to be more creative with it. Focus on your fifth chakra before beginning work, letting the energy flow and expand in a rich turquoise blue, out from your throat chakra and into the work you are about to create. Let go of any attachment to the outcome, for the sake of a purer creative urge from within. Allow the playful inner child to come out and enter into the creative process. Put your inner critic on hold while you work.

Don't limit your creativity to standard art forms. You can be creative in your dress, the route you take on your way to work, or the way you arrange your living space.

General Communication

Your work on this chakra should include efforts to communicate clearly wherever possible. If you find yourself repressing the urge to say something to someone, stop and examine your feelings. If you feel you are holding back for a good reason be very clear what your reason is. If not, try to bolster up your third chakra (personal power), take a deep breath, and say what you have to say. You will feel the purifying effects of good communication.

Journal Exercises

1. Communication

• What were the communication patterns in your family? Were you encouraged to speak your truth or discouraged? How was this done?

• How often were you listened to? Did you feel you were heard?

• Do you have trouble feeling heard now? What kind of response from a listener makes you feel heard?

• What are your fears in speaking out? Where in your body do you feel them?

• What muscles and thoughts do you use to keep yourself from talking when you feel shy? What chakras do you suppress in order to do this?

• Make a list of people important to you that you feel you have unfinished communication with. Go over in your mind what you want to say. See if there are similarities in content between what you want to say to each person. Is there a general topic that continually gets avoided? What are your fears around that topic? Finish communications where you can.

• A lot of communication is about listening to the inner voices. How well do you hear your inner voices and how well do they dialogue with each other?

2. The Fairy Tale

This exercise can be fun to write and gives us an archetypal perspective of the difficulties we suffered as children through circumstances of our birth, child abuse, parenting, and current situations.

Write about yourself as if you were writing a fairy tale, writing it in the third person. An example might be:

Once upon a time, in a land far, far away, there was a little girl who had no friends. She lived way out in the woods and had no brothers and sisters, and only a very sick Mommy and a very mean Daddy to talk to. She had to take care of her Mommy all day and cook for her Daddy each night.

One day, when the little girl was so sad and so lonely, she could hardly stand it..."

The story does not have to be entirely real, and you can make up characters and events that solve some of the problems you suffered. The result can trigger your own creativity in solving the problems and traumas of the past and the present.

3. Letter Writing

Unfinished communication can create blocks in the throat chakra. You can think of it as taking up room on the chakra disk. When the disk is too full, we have less room for more information. Ever notice how you can be preoccupied, talking to someone in your head, and not really listening to what's around you?

When possible, speak to the person directly and clean up or complete the communication. Unfortunately, this is not always possible. Sometimes the person is not open to listening, lives too far away, or is no longer living. Other times it simply scares us to talk, and getting our feelings down on paper can help us organize what we want to say.

Writing letters in these cases is best done in two stages, though sometimes only one stage is necessary.

The first stage is to write the letter for yourself—a completely uncensored, unedited stream of consciousness. This letter is not for mailing but simply to open up blocked communication. You can say anything you like and let out all the anger and fear that you might have.

Sometimes this stage is enough and you don't need to mail the letter. If your target is no longer living this may suffice. If you feel you can complete a communication transaction, however, it takes a second letter, revised from the first, that you could actually send. Be sure to include:

• Why you are choosing to communicate this way.

• What it is you need to say and why it is difficult (include your feelings and focus on statements that begin with "I").

• What it is you want in response to this communication, whether it be an answer, a change in someone's behavior, or just simply acknowledgment.

Let the letter sit on your altar at least one night, while you sleep on it before you mail it. Even if no response comes from your request, simply finishing your end of the communication can be very helpful and healing.

4. Automatic Writing

Automatic writing can help free up creativity and release communication blocks by accessing deeper levels of awareness that are normally suppressed by our conscious waking mind. This technique involves the writing of a story, thought, or feelings, or just simply "free-associating" by writing down single disjointed words that come to you as you focus on a certain topic. This can be an especially useful way to access the meaning of dreams.

In automatic writing it is useful, though not absolutely necessary, to start with a basic topic. You might be having conflicts about a job or relationship. Begin with a few words that describe this job or relationship and jot them down with space in between for further writing.

Then go back and freely write a few sentences next to each word—writing whatever comes into your mind as fast as you can. (You can also do this with a tape recorder if you feel the writing process is too slow.) Read it over the next day and see what themes emerge. You may want to write again on those themes.

5. Communicating with your Inner Child

As adults we have developed personalities to cope with the world and our day to day needs. Yet sometimes there are parts of us that are left behind in the day to day grind. There may be many parts to our being, but one part often overlooked is the Inner Child. The Inner Child represents aspects of ourselves whose development may have been arrested by trauma or abuse, or the forgotten playful, innocent part of ourselves. If we don't acknowledge the Inner Child, it can sabotage our adult behavior by suddenly acting childish in a relationship, behaving foolishly, or being overly needy. On the other hand, if we include the Inner Child in our decisions, then we can have the added enthusiasm of the child, the creativity and innocence that is very energizing.

Many people with traumatic childhoods have trouble finding or communicating with their inner child. One exercise that is helpful is to take a piece of paper, and divide it down the middle. Using your dominant hand on one side, write questions that you would like to ask your inner child. Using your other hand, write the answer, trying to write from a child's mind state. A typical conversation might look like this:

<u>adult</u>

1. How do you feel?
2. What are you scared of?
3. I like you. I think you're wonderful.
4. Why do you think that?
5. Do you feel abandoned when I work?
6. What would make you feel better?
7. OK, we'll play this afternoon, OK?

<u>Child</u>

1. Scared.
2. That no one will like me.
3. No you don't!
4. You work all the time.
5. Yeah.
6. Play with me.
7. I hope so!

Once you do this exercise a few times and establish contact, you may be able to do it internally at will.

6. Reassessment

• What have you learned about yourself as you've worked through the activities for the fifth chakra?

• What areas of this chakra do you need to work on? How will you do that?

• What areas of this chakra do you feel pleased with? How can you utilize these strengths?

Entering Sacred Space

Group Ritual
Materials Needed

Rattles and drums

Word Empowerment Circle

Form a circle and begin toning, each participant sounding in whatever way feels right to them. Listen as you are toning, and begin to find a way to blend the sounds, bringing the group energy together as your voices come together in a harmonious way. Allow the sound to find its completion and come to silence, listening to the quiet breathing of the group.

One at a time, participants enter the center of the circle and tell the group what they want to be told, what they want to remember. Phrase this simply, so that the group can chant the words back. Examples: You are loved, you are beautiful, your life is where it's supposed to be. Group members rattle and drum in rhythm with the chant, while the participant in the center soaks up the words and the energy.

Chanting Circle

One style commonly used in group circles is for each person in the circle to lead a song or a chant of their choosing and to pass the leadership around the circle so that everyone gets a turn. This does, however, require a repertoire of songs and chants to use. There is a small booklet of chants and songs called *The Green Earth Spirituality Songbook*, that is useful for such circles available from J. E. Shoup for $8 - 12 (sliding scale). Send your request to 2804 Hillegass, Berkeley, CA 94705. There are also tapes available with chants (see Resources).

Resources

Books

Bonny, Helen & Savary, Louis. *Music and your Mind*. Station Hill.

Drury, Nevill. *Music for Inner Space*. Prism Press.

Gardner-Gordon, Joy. *The Healing Voice*. The Crossing Press.

Goldberg, Natalie. *Writing Down the Bones*. Shambhala.

Goodman, Gerald & Esterly, Glenn. *The Talk Book*. Rodale Press.

Halpern, Steven. *Tuning the Human Instrument*. Spectrum Research.

Hamel, Peter Michael. *Through Music to the Self*. Shambhala.

Kealoha, Anna. *Songs of the Earth*. Celestial Arts.

McKay, Matthew, Davis, Martha & Fanning, Patrick. *Messages: The Communications Book*. New Harbinger.

Tannen, Deborah. *You Just Don't Understand*. Ballentine.

Music

Foundation for Shamanic Studies. Many shamanic tapes with a variety of instruments.

Gyuto Monks. *Tibetan Tantric Choir*.

Halpern, Steven. *Hear to Eternity*.

Hamouris, Deborah & Rick. *Welcome to Annwfn*. (Open Circle distributors, PO Box 773, Laytonville, CA 95454.)

Hart, Mickey. *Planet Drum*.
   At the Edge.

Lewis, Brent. *Earth Tribe Rhythms*. (Brent Lewis Productions, P.O. Box 461352, Los Angeles, CA 90046).

Libana. *A Circle is Cast*
   Fire Within

Prem Das & Muruga. *Journey of the Drum*.

Reclaiming Collective. *Chants: Ritual Music*. (Reclaiming Collective, P.O. Box 14404, San Francisco, CA 94114.)

Riley, Terry. *A Rainbow in Curved Air*.

Urubamba. *Good News for Pan Pipes*.

Wolff & Henning. *Tibetan Bells I & II*.

Ztiworoh, Drahcir. *Eros in Arabia*.

Chakra Six

Light

Getting Started

Where Are You Now?

Take time to reflect on the following concepts and write down whatever thoughts or phrases come to mind about how they operate in your life.

Light	*Dreams*
Darkness	*Memory*
Color	*Imagination*
Vision	*Visualization*
Beauty	*Clairvoyance*
Pattern	*Intuition*

This chakra involves the eyes and forehead. How do you feel about these areas of your body? Are there any difficulties you've had in these areas at any time during your life?

Altar Arrangement

Since this chakra's work deals largely with visual material, make your altar look especially pretty. You need not stick to the indigo color related to this chakra, but can explore color in all its rainbow variety. Arrange your crystals in a mandala pattern, with rainbow candles, colored scarves, artwork, flowers or photographs that you like. Use mirrors and candles that reflect both light and your own countenance, to remind you of the power of the image. Have fun and let your imagination run wild!

Correspondences	
Sanskrit name	Ajna
Meaning	To know, to perceive, to command
Location	Technically, the cave of Brahma, or the center of the head behind the eyebrows. Otherwise known as the brow chakra, the third eye is between the two physical eyes.
Element	Light
Main Issue	Visual perception, imagination, intuition, clairvoyance
Goals	Ability to perceive patterns, to "see"
Malfunction	Headaches, nightmares, hallucinations, poor visual perception
Color	Indigo
Planet	Neptune
Foods	None. Consciousness-altering substances.
Right	To See
Stones	Lapis lazuli, some quartz crystals
Animals	Owl, butterfly
Operating principle	Image formation
Yoga Path	Yantra yoga, the yoga of meditating on visual objects
Archetype	Hermit, Psychic, Dreamer

Sharing the Experience

"The most interesting thing for me this month has been paying attention to my dreams. I don't usually remember my dreams so I never paid much attention to them, but this month, in the process of keeping a dream journal, I found myself more tuned into them and better able to remember them. In doing so I learned a lot about myself."

•

"I spent this month looking at the division between what I can see and what I can say. My block is still in communication—I see a lot of things that I don't know how to put into words. So I found myself drawing and using non-verbal methods to express myself and that helped a lot."

•

"I took the opportunity of working on the sixth chakra to do something I like to do that I gave up a long time ago, and that's painting. I got out my paints, walled myself off in my room and started painting. It brought back a whole part of myself that I had forgotten about. As a result I have been more visually aware, looking more carefully at things, seeing how the colors and shapes go together."

"I'm in the midst of a lot of change. I'm not sure how to put it into sixth chakra context, but I guess I see myself growing out of an old pattern, and wanting to create a new pattern but not yet sure how. I am trying to visualize how that would work, but I'm having a hard time seeing it, or maybe just a hard time believing in it."

•

"I had a grand vision this month. I was part of an all-night ceremonial vision quest, for which I prepared with purification, fasting, and sweat-lodge the night before. Towards the end of the night, there was a group journey to the future to look for guidance in helping us get from here to there. I saw in the future a vision of global consciousness, a sense of the consciousness net having connected all the way around the globe and being connected with the earth. It was staggering and very encouraging."

Understanding the Concept

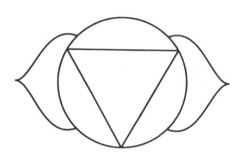

Chakra Six, located at the forehead, is also known as the third eye. Symbolized by a lotus with only two petals, visualize it as a deep indigo blue. This is the center of *visual, psychic* and *intuitive perception*—the place where we store our memories, perceive our dreams, and imagine our future.

At chakra five we experienced the wavelike emission of sound and its ability to carry information through symbols such as words. At chakra six we experience the perception of a wavelike phenomenon of a higher octave—that of light and its ability to bring us information in the form of *colors and images*.

Seeing

This chakra is about seeing. As the internal mental screen upon which we project all our visual images from memory, dreams, clairvoyance and imagination, this chakra is the center that *receives, stores, interprets, creates, and projects visually encoded information.* Its name, *Ajna*, means both to perceive and to command. A visualization held strongly is the first step in bringing an ethereal thought-form into manifestation. We can take command of our lives through the images we hold in our minds.

Psychic Abilities

The *Ajna* chakra is associated with psychic and intuitive abilities, most specifically *clairvoyance*. Clairvoyance, from the French, meaning "clear seeing," is the ability to see clearly through the limitations of space and time and perceive energetic patterns such as the chakras and the aura, information from the future (precognition), or information from a distant location (remote viewing). It is the ability to perceive and interpret from one's own mind images that contain valid information about a person, place, or situation.

Intuition, a more subtle psychic quality, is the ability to see or sense a situation through non-logical means, as in "intuitive leaps," termed (appropriately) *insight*, although intuition does not always involve the perception of an internal visual image. All of us have and use intuition as a part of our daily lives. Many people are at least partially clairvoyant, and basic psychic abilities can be developed by anyone willing to put forth the time and energy toward developing them.

Patterns

Learning to see involves the ability to perceive and recognize patterns. Patterns reveal the underlying order of things. Through the understanding of a pattern we can predict what the next piece of the puzzle might be. Seeing is about recognition, or the process of re-cognizing or re-knowing. When we finally understand something we say, "Oh, I see!" meaning that we recognize the pattern—it reverberates with previously perceived patterns in our consciousness. The ability to see, whether it is right here and now in the physical world, or clairvoyantly seeing something in a future time or distant place, is all a matter of recognizing pattern. We can say, "I remember what happened last time I saw this and if I know what's good for me, I'd better be careful!" and we are recognizing a pattern and predicting a possible future. Clairvoyance is a process of recognizing subtler patterns in the fabric of our reality.

Most of us tend to look at a pattern until we recognize it. If we see someone walking down the street that looks vaguely familiar we look at them until we "recognize" them and say, "Oh, that's Jackie," and then we stop looking for more details. We usually stop "seeing" at that point, meaning we stop pursuing new information. What it takes to open the third eye is the development of the ability to look past our usual stopping point. It's how deeply we are willing to "look" at something that determines how much we see. To really "look" we need to let go of our preconceived patterns and see freshly, taking in new details and being open to the perception of new patterns. This requires practices that help clean the mind of old patterns and images, such as meditation.

Memory

We store the experiences of our past as patterns in *memory*. Memory comes to consciousness as a projection of stored images (or sensations) upon the third eye screen. If you decide you are going to sit back and remember your first apartment, you are calling up that image and projecting it upon your inner screen. Here you can view it in 3-dimensional technicolor and re-experience all the associated feelings and sensations. Our memory works much like a hologram: each fragment reflects the whole picture, with the resolution getting clearer with each piece we add. (For a more detailed description of holograms and third eye functioning, see *Wheels of Life*, pp. 328-333.)

Internal Viewing

We project onto our screen images of imagination, fantasy, dreams, and intuition. When we meet someone, we might project our "pictures" from past relationships, adapted to the new situation, or plug our new person straight into our fantasies. It is important to note that *whether we are looking at something imagined or remembered, the internal viewing process is largely the same.* This can make it difficult to tell the difference between memory and imagination, which may get confused. The good news, however, is that if you have the ability to remember visually, you can probably learn to develop clairvoyant skills as well. Both involve the ability to visualize, the ability to retrieve information and to play it upon the internal screen. The difference depends on the question—whether it is a question of the past where we excavate the image from memory, or whether from the future, created from imagination. There is no guarantee, of course, that an image created from imagination in answer to a question will necessarily give you the right answer, but it provides a method of getting information. Check all answers out empirically to see if they are valid. Through the feedback we get from checking our answers afterward, we begin to learn the difference between self-created imagination-based information and true precognition, clairvoyance, or remote viewing.

We also project pictures onto the future based on the past which influence our behavior. We project a picture that this relationship will never work out, this job is a rip-off, that we are not safe, or worthy. If I go to a job interview with the picture that I won't be hired, I will be nervous and apologetic and make a less favorable impression. If I have the picture that they are going to love me I will perform quite differently and create a more favorable outcome. The power of our perceptions has the ability to command our reality thus relating to the two meanings of the word *ajna:* to perceive and to command.

Transcendence

As we move up the chakras, we are getting broader in our scope. We move away from specific details and into meta-patterns. From this perspective the lower chakra patterns appear as subroutines. In the upper chakras we transcend the normal limitations of time and space. We can remember what we did last week or ten years ago as well as imagine what we'd like to do next summer. The movement upward is the movement of transcendence, the movement down is of immanence. Through transcendence we learn to stretch beyond our limitations; we can achieve a bit of distance that may allow us to see from a different perspective.

Chakra Six, then, is where we can transcend the limitations imposed on us by physicality and enter new realms of imagination. We develop new ways of obtaining information, thus expanding our consciousness to ever deeper and broader levels of understanding, such as the mythic realm, a world of rich symbolism. It takes a "stilling" of the constant train of images and thoughts from the conscious mind to perceive the mythic realm. Meditation is one tool for achieving this; other tools commonly used throughout history are ritual, psychoactive substances, and dreams.

Dreams

Dreams allow us to enter into the timeless world of archetypal symbolism. Our dreams take us on a visually encoded symbolic journey through our unconscious, our emotions, and our spiritual life. Each image in a dream is rich with meaning. Each image combines memory and imagination and enacts a drama of relationships between patterns, allowing a new order to emerge if we can allow ourselves to open to it. Dreams are the unconscious cataloguing of patterns, images and emotions. Working with our dreams helps to develop the Ajna chakra, and to encounter our rich world of inner symbolism.

The deeper symbolic archetypal level reveals many aspects of our lives. Once we can stay still in that center, the patterns start to become clear. We can use meditation as a tool to penetrate our dreams as well as a tool for centering the mind and viewing with less attachment the constant run of images that flow through our consciousness at every moment.

Light & Color

The creation of pictures from the abstract realm of thought is the first step downward from the top in the path of manifestation. Before we can bring anything into being, we need to have a picture in our mind of what we are trying to create. I like to think of the rainbow as the first manifestation of light on its way to darkness because, as soon as light hits matter, it breaks up into colors. Light and color are significant aspects of the sixth chakra, for they are the means through which images reach our consciousness.

The seven chakras are often correlated with the seven colors of the rainbow: red, orange, yellow, green, blue, indigo, violet. The first chakra, which is the slowest vibration, is red light, which is the slowest frequency of the visual spectrum. The second chakra is orange, and each color progresses in order to the crown chakra which corresponds to violet—the fastest vibration in the visible spectrum. Visualizing these colors in meditations for cleansing the chakras is a simple tool that not only helps us get in touch with our chakras, but develops visualizing abilities as well. We include a meditation based on this idea on page 237.

Excess and Deficiency

Excess and deficiency are harder to ascertain in the upper two chakras. As they are oriented towards mental states, they are not as observable as behaviors in the lower chakras. Also, because our culture is somewhat skeptical of "psychism" and "higher consciousness," we have to weed out a cultural bias when we examine what is excessive or deficient.

Generally speaking, excess in chakra six would appear as aberrant psychism—paranoid fantasies, nightmares, hallucinations, and an inability to sort out appropriate responses to intuitive material. An example would be someone who picks up on a friend's anger, assumes it is directed towards herself, and acts accordingly, without checking it out first. Using communication to verify psychic intuition helps to ground it in reality. Some people experience being bombarded by psychic stimuli, and find it difficult to "see straight" because they cannot sort through all the input they are receiving. This can be seen as an inability to shield, and first chakra grounding techniques can help create a stronger container.

A deficient sixth chakra can result in insensitivity. A person may be completely oblivious to the subtleties around them. These are the people who "can't take a hint," and may need to be told explicitly what's going on before they are able to respond. They may be unable to imagine new ideas, or may denigrate others' attunement to dreams, intuitive insights, or imagination. Difficulty in seeing anything that is not right in front of you is a deficiency in the ability to visualize and project.

Images

Outside of our own imaginations, the images that surround and rule us are a major factor in shaping mass consciousness. Television, billboards, clothing trends, cinematography, and other visual media feed directly into our consciousness and become part of the storehouse of memory images that affect how we think and feel. To clear the chakra it is important to empty our minds of these images so that we can once again perceive with a freshness and clarity of vision. Only then can we begin to see accurately on the psychic planes. And when we do, we discover an exciting world of patterns and colors unlike anything in the physical realm.

Working with Movement

Archetype Dances

In our workshop, we bring many decks of Tarot and other archetypal symbols to the sixth chakra session. Choose a deck with images you are drawn to. Spread it out face up and look at the images. Choose a card that you feel attracted to.

Begin by closing your eyes and focusing on your breathing, allowing your body to relax. Imagine a blank screen in your mind. Now open your eyes and look at the card you have chosen. Don't worry about what the image is "supposed" to mean, just "be" with the image. What impressions do you get as you let the image in? Notice your feeling state as you look at the image. What feelings come up for you? What drew you to this image?

Form your body into a statue pose that expresses some of what you see or feel in the picture. This does not need to be a recreation of the pose of a figure on the card, although it might be. It's more important to find a way to embody your sense of what is going on in the picture. When you've found the pose that feels right, allow a movement to begin. This may be a very subtle movement or it may be a large forceful movement. It may be a repetitive, rhythmic movement, or it may be fits and starts. Begin to play with that movement, following it as it changes form and shifts. See where it is going, stay with it, holding your sense of the image as it moves you. Imagine that you've taken that image into your body and now you are seeing what resonates from within you. Notice how it feels to be moving this way, to be doing the dance of this image. Are the feelings you had before intensifying? Perhaps there are new feelings emerging as you explore the image from the inside out through your body. Let the dance change and flow with whatever emerges.

Group Work: Moving Dreamwork

This is a technique for exploring dreams in depth in a group, although a modified version could be done with just two people. One person's dream becomes the focus, and the dreamer begins by reading or telling the dream to the group. The dreamer chooses others in the group to play roles that appear in the dream, and this can include things as well as people. If the group is large and the dream has only one or two people or creatures in it, several people might take on a role from the environment, like the ocean, or the forest, or parts of the old house. Anything that appears in the dream can be part of the re-creation of it.

The re-creation can stay true to the dream, or the dreamer may change it to create a different outcome. Often, changes take place the second time through, after the dreamer and the group take time to share feelings and reactions from the re-creation of the dream as it was. Group members might have ideas that came to them as they played their roles about changes that might happen, and these can be incorporated.

This exercise is only partially for the sake of the dreamer. Many times group members find that similar themes to their own dreams emerge, and the dream reenactment may become something that all the participants experience as their own.

Putting It Into Practice

Here we are at chakra six, the chakra of light, color, image, imagination, intuition, vision, and dreams. Rising out of the realms of the body and heading deeper into the mind, we reach now into the psychic realms of perception, intuition and visualization.

Pay special attention to how things *look*, and to how the way they look affects you. This can be anything from how your looks affect how you feel, to how you feel about others, your home, a bit of scenery, an advertisement or a piece of art. Also pay attention to how others respond to the way you look and how you respond to the way they look.

Try to create a feeling of harmony and beauty in your physical surroundings. The third eye closes down when what we look at is unattractive or upsetting and opens up when sights around us are pleasing.

Give your eyes a feast. Take a trip to the country, to an art museum, to a visually stimulating film. Expose yourself to light and color and images. Take a journey through old photo albums and see what the images evoke.

Dreams

Pay special attention to your dreams, perhaps starting a dream journal or at least making an effort to write down your dreams. Dreams are the psyche's communication through visual symbols. They depict a pattern that represents the relationships of different aspects of your personality and purpose. Here is the third eye at work, untainted by the conscious mind. The symbols that appear have special information to relay to you for the enhancement and conscious recognition of your emotional and spiritual life. Here are some suggestions for working with your dreams.

Notice the symbols that repeatedly appear. Write them down, fantasize about them, create dialogue with your dream characters, or draw pictures. How do they relate to events in your life right now, especially current conflicts? What archetypal energies do they represent? How does that archetypal energy manifest in your life? How would you like it to manifest? How could you use that energy better? What are the emotional themes? Are you frequently scared, excited, quiet, running or still? Is your behavior in dreams very different from your waking life or an extension of it? If it is different, the dream may be revealing repressed aspects of yourself that you now have the opportunity to reclaim.

Problems in Dreaming

"I don't remember any of my dreams." This is a common complaint when you are not terribly connected to the sixth chakra. It does not mean that you don't dream, but that you do not bring your dream consciousness into waking consciousness. Sometimes the dream is so nonsensical to the conscious mind it's as if it were in a different language and it is automatically dismissed. Sometimes the conscious mind is not ready to confront the repressed material revealed in the dream. Other times it is merely an undeveloped habit, a result of paying too little attention to our dreams. Here are a few suggestions:

Before you go to sleep give yourself a suggestion that you will remember at least one aspect of a dream. It could be a word, an image, a symbol or a feeling. When you begin to awaken be sure to stay in the same position as when you were just asleep. Keep your eyes closed and avoid even wiggling a finger if you can. If you have moved to turn off the alarm, return to your former position as quickly as possible. See what images come to consciousness. Don't try to analyze them, simply focus on them. After you have mentally reviewed all that you can remember, write or draw in your journal whatever has come to mind, moving as little as possible. This is best done before speaking to anyone, going to the bathroom or getting dressed. If nothing has come to mind, write your thoughts or feelings upon waking anyway, as they may be the vestiges of a dream you just had but can't recall. Start small and when you can retrieve one thing you can expand to retrieving whole segments of dreams.

If writing in a dream journal becomes a frequent activity upon waking, you will find that you automatically begin to remember more dreams and have a richer dream life. It is useful to keep a diary of the images and symbols that parade through and read it often, watching for repeating patterns and symbols.

Dream Analysis

There are numerous books on dream analysis that may give you tables of symbols and tell you what they mean, but we recommend that you stay away from them. It is more important to explore what the dream symbol means to you and how it relates to your life, past, present and future. As the unconscious mind creates each piece of the dream, it is valuable to regard each piece as an aspect of your own self. This includes inanimate objects such as cars or houses, as well as threatening characters such as demons or criminals. A common dream, for example, might be that you are riding in a car that is going too fast or one that runs out of gas. If the car represents an aspect of you, then you might determine that it is telling you that you are going too fast or that you are running out of energy.

Most often our shadow side, or aspects of our personality that we have repressed, will show up in dreams in a frightening form. We can transform these shadow aspects when we meet them with understanding rather than fear or aggression. Talking to the scary character that is chasing you instead of running, or imagining that you are that character, can begin to penetrate its meaning. Create dialogues in your journal between aspects of the dream—where the car talks to the house or where the dark pursuer talks to the victim, until you gain some resolution or insight. Often the dreams we remember are dreams that are interrupted by alarm clocks or noise and taking time to complete them in a semi-wakened state can help resolve whatever issues the dream was trying to express.

Lucid Dreaming

Lucid dreaming is the ability to realize you are dreaming without waking up, and to take conscious action in your dreams. In lucid dreaming you can decide to confront a scary figure, change a symbol or create a new dream image, while you are still asleep. To work your way into lucid dreaming you can begin with the suggestion to yourself as you fall asleep that you intend to have a lucid dream. In the early morning go over your dream without moving until you have memorized it. Again, give yourself the suggestion, saying, "Next time I'm dreaming I want to remember to realize I am dreaming." Then visualize yourself returning to the dream you just had, only this time visualize yourself realizing you are dreaming, and see yourself taking an active part in it. Repeat these steps until you fall asleep or until they are very fixed in your mind. You may also wish to add a calming suggestion to your lucid dream command. Often when we are first successful at lucid dreaming we get so excited we wake ourselves up! It is important to let that part of the conscious mind simply be a quiet observer, so as not to alter the dreaming state. It is also recommended in lucid dreaming that you do not change the dream too much or you will shatter the dream and wake up. Stephen LaBerge, author of the book *Lucid Dreaming,* says it is better to "control yourself, not your dreams." His suggestions are to spin, turn around, or fall backward in your dream self. Others have found that simply blinking may help to change a scene.

Visualization Exercises

The practice of visualization aids in the development of the sixth chakra.

Colors

Begin your practice of visualization with simple color. The chakras correspond to a rainbow progression of colors, from top to bottom: violet, indigo, blue, green, yellow, orange, red. Your meditation might involve visualizing light in each of these colors in turn, flooding the particular chakra associated with that color. Imagine pulling each color out of an infinite supply of white light, as white is the combination of all colors. Visualize yourself and the chakras as the prism that light passes through on its way to manifestation. (Note: If you can only do one exercise this month, this would be the one to practice.)

Forms

Practice visualizing forms with simple exercises such as visualizing a glass and then imagining it filling with water. Practice visualizing squares, circles, or other shapes, and imagine them changing color or size.

Images

You can then practice with images, thinking of the things you are trying to manifest in your life right now and visualizing them as if they were already here. For example, you might want to imagine yourself going to your new job, wearing your new clothes, sitting and talking with your new lover. You might imagine the balance of your checkbook with an extra zero at the end, or imagine your house painted or cleaned, or imagine your body looking different. The daily visualization of your dreams helps to bring them into reality.

Questions

Use visualization to answer questions that you are struggling with (or at least give hints). Sit quietly in meditation and allow your mind to enter a blank state. Clear your visual screen and let it go dark. Then ask your question and allow images to form in your mind. This works very much like dreams—the images may be mysterious representatives of psychological aspects of your dilemma rather than direct answers. You must then derive the answer from the images.

Another technique is to imagine a gauge on your visual screen. The gauge can go from 0 to 100, or from yes to no, or from this job to that job, or whatever fits your question. Pose your question and without deciding intellectually where the gauge should fall, simply allow it to fall where it may and observe the information it gives you. You might ask, "How productive will this job be for me?" and the gauge will swing somewhere between 0 and 100. Or "Should I move to a new city or not?" and the gauge would work on its yes/no axis. The idea is to let your subconscious mind answer the question rather than your conscious mind.

Photo Blink

This exercise is a simple way to get a sense of someone's aura if you normally don't see auras. It also helps to improve visual observation.

Stand directly opposite the person you want to look at, about six feet away. Close your eyes and clear your mental screen. Wait until you feel grounded and centered, with no particular thoughts or images running across your mind. Just once, quickly open and close your eyes again—the opposite of a blink—so that you get only a quick glimpse of the person in front of you, imprinting a frozen "photographic image" in your mind's eye. Hold that image and examine it. What characteristics stand out? Do you see an afterimage or glow around the body? Do certain colors or body positions stand out? As the image fades, quickly open and close your eyes again to strengthen it. See how much detail you can decipher in this afterimage. Which parts fade first and which linger the longest? All these things tell you about the strength and weakness of the person's aura.

Meditation

The path of meditation for this chakra is called *yantra yoga*, which is meditation using a mandala or other visual object as a tool for centering the mind. On the page opposite is a black and white mandala. As this chakra focuses on color and image, try photocopying and coloring this mandala in colors that you resonate with and then use it as a meditation device, quietly gazing upon it, centering yourself, and breathing deeply.

Psychic work

The development of psychic abilities is the outgrowth of work on the sixth chakra. Associated with clairvoyance or "clear seeing," this chakra works with visual symbols as a communication system. Through the development of our power to visualize, we simultaneously develop the ability to see psychically.

Aura Reading

Anyone can do basic aura reading. Through practice we can become good at it.

Sit opposite someone and take a close look at them. Look at the way they hold their body, the colors they wear, the tone of their complexion. Look for the parts of them that seem to have the most energy or presence. Look at the parts that appear held back or frozen or void of energy. Begin to look at how these places connect and imagine the pathways energy would take to pass through this person's body. Imagine that you are seeing a traffic pattern in the shape of their body. How would your traffic report read?

Next try the same exercise with your eyes closed. Some people find it helps to hold a hand up, palm facing the person you are reading, to help sense the energy. Notice what images come to your own mind. Begin by just reporting those images to the person you are "reading," even if they seem to make no sense. You might get an image of red, or an image of a dog, or of a car driving down the road. Without practice and training there is no way to guarantee that what you are seeing is a clairvoyant perception of their aura or your own imagination, but when you report the images to the person you are working with they can comment on whether it's relevant to their lives at the time, and through the feedback you begin to learn the difference between "clear seeing" and imagination. Clairvoyant images are usually stronger and have a sense of appearing on their own—they seem to come out of the person we are viewing rather than our own heads.

Intuition

There are many books full of psychic exercises, but there are few things more helpful than simply using your intuition in every case possible and checking out the results. For example, take a moment before you answer the phone and see if you can sense who is calling. Try to imagine what colors a friend might wear that you are about to see. Project an image of someone you would like to hear from or run into and see if you can make it happen. Each time you are correct the feedback will strengthen your confidence in your psychic abilities, which in turn strengthens the abilities themselves.

Chakra Drawing

It is possible to do a reading on your own chakras through creating a visual representation of your inner experience. This has been a favorite part of our classes and the sharing of drawings amongst each other always shows the incredible variety of possible expression. The only materials needed are one or two large sheets of newsprint (18" x 24" is best) per person, and a box of crayons or colored chalk. It is not necessary to have artistic abilities.

Take some time to go into a meditative state. Allow your mind to become blank, clearing your visual screen of distractions, preconceptions, or expectations of yourself as an artist. When you feel ready to begin, tune into your first chakra and allow an image to form that expresses the patterns of energy that reside there. It might feel open or closed, bright or dark, ethereal and full of soft swirls, or dense and full of heavy squares and angles. It is important to get away from what your chakras are *supposed* to look like—don't pick red because it is the color of the first chakra unless it fits with your inner experience.

When you have a sense of the pattern, reach for the crayons and draw it at the bottom of the paper.

Then go inside and view your second chakra in the same way. When you have a sense of it, begin to draw its form on your paper above the second chakra. Repeat, one chakra at a time until you get to the crown. (Do it from the top down if you prefer.)

When you are finished, look at the drawing as a whole. What kind of impression do you get about this person? Are the chakras connected to each other? Are some chakras noticeably bigger or smaller than others? If this drawing was all you knew about someone, what advice might you give them about balancing their chakras?

Visual Creativity

Gather some old magazines with pictures that appeal to you and assemble a collage on a large piece of paper or cardboard. Don't worry about why you are choosing each picture or why you are placing it on the page, just follow your own aesthetic. After you have finished put your collage up somewhere you can see it daily and let insights about it come as you ponder your creation over time.

Imagination

Use your imagination. Don't do things in the same old familiar ways. Imagine something new. Dress imaginatively, do something unusual, draw or paint a picture, create a colorful display with flowers, food, clothing, or doodles in your journal. Above all, have fun!

Journal Exercises

1. Pattern Recognition

Notice the patterns running through your life—in your relationships, in your behavior, in your family dynamics. An example of a family pattern might be that you are anxious at mealtimes because your family used to fight at those times. Perhaps you separated from your significant other at the same age your parents were when they separated. You may notice that you continue to choose partners who have some of the same characteristics despite vowing never to do that again! If you have kept a journal, you may read over the same themes again and again, perhaps with slight variations each time, and wonder "Why does this always happen to me?"

Often, we repeat patterns until we understand what drives us to repeat them and address the underlying issues. This is not an overnight process, but we can approach it by exploring the origins of the patterns we carry through our lives and by looking for the meanings they hold.

To begin this process, ask yourself the following questions:

• What patterns do I currently engage in that do not serve me in the best possible way?

• Who in my past exhibited similar patterns? How did that affect me?

• When is the first time I remember doing this, and what events, feelings, and thoughts do I associate with that time?

• What was/is my underlying need that prompts this pattern?

• How else could I address that underlying need?

• What new pattern can I envision that would be more appropriate?

2. Image

• What image do I have of myself physically?

• How important do I make my appearance and my attachment to physical image for myself?

Journal Exercises

- How much do I assume about or judge others by their image?

- What image do I want people to have of me?

- How does this compare with the feedback I get from others?

- What sacrifices have I made, or am I willing to make, to project a certain image?

- Who are the people in my life with whom I have no need to project an image? How do I feel with them?

3. Dream Journal

Journal writing can be an excellent way to access meaning from your dreams. You may want to keep a special journal just for dreams and dreamwork and keep it by your bed, or you could keep your dreamwork along with your other journal in one place. We include more details about dreamwork in the tasks section.

4. Visuals

A picture is worth a thousand words. You do not have to limit your journal to words and writing. Feel free to draw and to paste pictures from magazines, or photos to stimulate your visual senses. Allow your journal to take on more of a pictorial quality.

5. Reassessment

- What have you learned about yourself as you've worked through the activities for the sixth chakra?

- What areas of this chakra do you need to work on? How will you do that?

- What areas of this chakra do you feel pleased with? How can you utilize these strengths?

Entering Sacred Space

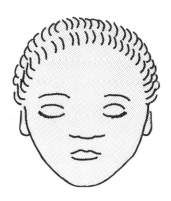

Creating your Inner Temple

This journey can be taken alone or in a group. One person can lead the other participants through the journey or you can tape it and play it back. Participants may want to be in a comfortable position and stay in it throughout the journey, but some may find it more effective to move with eyes closed, allowing their bodies to re-enact some of the motions visualized. The preparation is useful for any trance journey you would like to embark on, and you are only limited by your imagination.

Close your eyes and allow your body to enter deep relaxation (see Introductory chapter). Imagine that you are in your room at home in the dark, and you become aware that, at the back of your closet, there is a doorway. Go to that doorway and step through to a stairway that spirals down. At first it is very dark and you go by feel, touching each step down carefully with your toes before placing your weight on the step. Work your way down the stairs until you come to the bottom, where your feet touch sand and you hear water sounds. Follow the sound to the edge of a large body of water, with a boat that you can climb into, arrayed with comfortable cushions. As you settle yourself into the boat, it drifts away from shore and you know it is taking you to a special place, a place that will have everything you need for exploring your inner worlds. Let the boat carry you, rocking you through the waters, to that place, and on the way look around you, noticing what you see. What sort of place are you traveling through? Is it light or dark or in between? Can you see the sky or something else? Are there any creatures along the way?

As you come to your temple, notice the surroundings. How do you enter? Are there others here? Your temple space may be indoors or outdoors, or something in between, but it is defined in some way, the edges of your space are defined. Notice those edges now, moving around the perimeter of your space with your body or your eyes. What is here in this space with you? Is there anything else you need here? Whatever you need, just ask for it. Everything is available to you. Spend some time here, doing what you need to do to be comfortable, to make this space yours. If there is someone you would like to be here with you, animal, human, or something else, either someone you already know or someone you would like to get to know, you may invite them to join you.

When you feel finished, say your farewells to the space and anyone who joined you, and find your way back to the boat that is waiting for you on the water. Climb in and return the way you came, allowing the boat to take you back to the shore where the spiral stairs lead up to your room. Make your way back, climbing those stairs up and entering your room through the closet. When you are there, bring your attention back to your body, here in this room, beginning to breathe deeper, bringing in oxygen and energy and letting it spread throughout your body, awakening each cell, each muscle. Begin to move gently, stretching, yawning, however your body needs to move to bring your awareness fully back into the physical body. When you're ready, open your eyes and write in your journal whatever you want to remember. You might even draw your temple space or anything else that seemed important. If you are in a group, share your experiences, then ground the circle together.

Resources

Books

Capacchione, Lucia. *Lighten Up Your Body—Lighten Up Your Life*. Newcastle Pub.

Cunningham, Scott. *Sacred Sleep*. The Crossing Press.

Greer, Mary. *Tarot for Your Self*. Newcastle.

Houston, Jean & Masters, Robert. *Mind Games*.

Hutchinson, Marcia. *Transforming Body Image*. Crossing Press.

LaBerge, Steven. *Lucid Dreaming*. Ballantine.

Mariechild, Diane. *Motherwit: A Guide to Healing & Psychic Development*. The Crossing Press.

Samuels, Mike & Nancy. *Seeing with the Mind's Eye*. Random House.

Targ, Russell & Harary, Keith. *The Mind Race: Understanding and Using Psychic Abilities*. Villard Books.

Tucci, Guiseppe. *The Theory and Practice of the Mandala*. Weiser.

Chakra Seven
Thought

Getting Started

Where Are You Now?

Write down your thoughts about the following concepts:

Consciousness	*Divinity*
Awareness	*God*
Learning	*Goddess*
Intelligence	*Spirit*
Information	*Emptiness*

This chakra involves the cerebral cortex. We are in realms that are less physical, so instead of asking about your head, it is more appropriate to ask how you feel about your mind. This involves how you regard yourself as a thinking being, how you relate to your mental capacities, what problems you may experience.

Altar Arrangement

The color of this chakra is violet, though many people think of it as white, which is a combination of all the colors. Try combining the two using white and violet flowers, perhaps a lavender scarf over a white altar cloth. The Hindu God Shiva is connected with the crown chakra—his lightning bolt comes out of his head and destroys ignorance. Since this chakra is the thousand-petaled lotus, an appropriate image can be made with many-petaled flowers floating in a bowl of water.

The seventh chakra represents emptiness on the material plane, so an altar would not have very much on it. A simple cloth with a single candle and an occasional flower are plenty. You could also add a mirror to remind you of the Divinity within.

Correspondences

Sanskrit name	Sahasrara
Meaning	Thousandfold
Location	Top of head, cerebral cortex
Element	Thought
Main Issue	Understanding
Goals	Expanded consciousness
Malfunction	*Deficient:* Depression, alienation, confusion, boredom, apathy, inability to learn or comprehend. *Excessive:* Overly intellectual, heady, spacey.
Color	Violet
Planet	Uranus
Foods	None, fasting
Right	To Know
Stones	Amethyst, diamond
Animals	Elephant, ox, bull
Operating principle	Consciousness
Yoga Path	Jnana yoga, meditation
Archetype	Sage, Wisewoman, Shiva

Sharing the Experience

"Getting to the seventh chakra step by step has been a new experience for me. I had always worked from my crown down, but I never worked from the ground up. And everything was always white. Now I see all the colors. It was a big change to come from that heavy ground place. At each step I actually opened that area. It started working and moving and affecting my life! I got a loving relationship, I got my business moving and changing. I moved to the power area and I was able to get angry. Usually I just go out of my body, but I couldn't do that anymore. I found myself blocked in communications, then they started opening up. It took nurturing that little child to break it up. But now I have a whole different understanding. So my report is less on the seventh chakra than on the whole experience."

•

"I spent a lot of time this month examining my thinking processes. I've come to realize how much self-programming I do with running negative thoughts—'you're not good enough, no one will like what you have to say, you don't know what you're talking about.' I made a real effort to examine where those mental tapes came from and to turn them into something more positive and it's really made a difference. I've been learning to understand instead of judge."

•

"I used this month to make myself meditate. I've always done it haphazardly, ten minutes here, skip a few days, ten minutes there. Since this is the chakra we were working on, I made it a point to meditate for a full fifteen minutes each morning before I did anything else. At this point it is starting to become a habit—the only time I didn't do it was on a weekend where I went out of town, and I missed it. Strangely enough, even though this chakra is on the upper end of things, the meditation has made me feel more grounded. I hope that I continue the process now that the Intensive is over."

•

"I read a lot of books this month. Usually I read a lot of science fiction which I really enjoy, but I don't stick with non-fiction books. It's always felt too intellectual. But this month I delved into a bunch of things—psychology books, modern philosophy, new physics—real heady stuff. Strangely enough I enjoyed it and feel like less of a bimbo intellectually. I think I'll try to keep a more balanced ratio between fiction and non-fiction from now on."

•

"I did a lot of reading this month too, mostly delving into Joseph Campbell and examining myths and archetypes. I tried to sort out the archetypal influences in my life and see what archetypes my friends embodied. I also looked at my dreams from this perspective and learned a lot. It gave me a certain detachment from my problems that allowed me to see them in a different light. I don't know if I have the answers yet, but this seems to have changed the questions."

●

"I tried to focus on meditation but wasn't as successful as Frank. I found my body kept distracting me—I would get a muscle ache, or an itch, or I'd be cold or hot. So I used the breathing exercises from the fourth chakra to help me get calm and focused and allowed those to be my meditation. I think it left me feeling more clear-headed, which I guess has some seventh-chakra correlation. But for me there is a lot I have to work out in my body and it is more important to focus there. That's what my seventh chakra thinking tells me anyway!"

●

"I worked with the concept of just knowing, in the sense of trying to trust my own inner wisdom. My father had always made me defend myself by making me prove I was right and he was always better at it than me, so I learned to distrust my own inner voice unless it was extremely rational. So this month I learned to listen to my less rational voices and to find hidden wisdom within them. To learn to understand the basis for some of my feelings and that something can be true, even if I can't prove it empirically, has been a growing experience."

Understanding the Concept

We are now at the height of our chakra column, the thousand petaled lotus blooming serenely out of the crown chakra at the top of our heads. This chakra relates to *thought, consciousness, information,* and *intelligence.* Like the roots branching out of our base chakra, tendrils of consciousness branch out from the crown chakra, perceiving, analyzing, and assimilating infinite bits of information, each enfolded into our ever-growing matrix of understanding. This chakra is concerned with the way we think, our belief systems, and our connection to higher power.

Thought

The crown chakra relates to the process of *knowing*, just as the other chakras have been about seeing, hearing or feeling. We look at the way we think—both content and pattern—and ask the questions, "How do we know what we know?" and "Who or what is it that does the knowing?" The answer to this question is the very consciousness that we seek to understand, embody, and enhance. Our task here is to examine our thoughts, our beliefs, and our process of receiving, analyzing and storing information—the examination of consciousness itself.

We have introduced the concept of a chakra as analogous to a floppy disk used in a computer, with each chakra containing a specific program about how to run our lives. Using this analogy, the crown chakra can be seen as the disk that contains the *operating system* for the entire mind-body biocomputer. Our core beliefs determine the operating system we have. If I believe that everyone is out to get me, then I will perceive information through a paranoid operating system and behave accordingly. If I believe the world is a benevolent place, I am more likely to operate in a way that supports that—and subsequently continue to perceive it as benevolent. In other words, the world often behaves the way we think it will—and that's why.

Thought, the element associated with the crown chakra, is the first emanation of consciousness on its way to manifestation. We can conceptualize thought as the seed of manifestation—the blueprint that gives form to all that is created. To see what consciousness looks like, we need only look around us. All that we see is the manifestation of consciousness, whether it be a building created out of an architect's imagination, a tree growing towards the sunlight, or an animal looking for food.

But what is this elusive thing called consciousness and what does it do?

Order

To the Hindus, the one underlying reality in this transient world is order. Even if we consider the world an illusion, we must admit that it is a very ordered illusion. The planets travel around the sun in a precise manner, Earth regulates Her own atmosphere, and precision dominates the gross physical universe. It is this order that enables us, through our consciousness, to perceive pattern— we recognize a flower, a face, or a voice by its pattern.

Order is pattern perceived from the view of a particular point of consciousness, which is in itself ordered in a unique way. The order that a honeybee perceives from the viewpoint of its consciousness is vastly different from our own and so is the information each of us derives from the same set of circumstances. As we are patterned, so do we perceive.

Each of us, from our unique point of view, creates an internal "matrix" which is the structural core of our conscious ordering system. In simple terms, we could call this matrix our belief systems, but it is much more than that. This core is created throughout our lifetime, particularly childhood, as our nervous and muscular systems are developing. The core matrix then gets "hard-wired" into our system and may be beyond our conscious control, though not unchangeable if we choose to examine it. Someone who is physically abused, for example, may have in their core matrix a pattern of fear and defensiveness even when they are in the presence of a trusted person who they do not "believe" will harm them. It becomes part of their unconscious belief system, and its constellated pattern (rapid heartbeat, tight stomach, etc.) has become "habit," and needs to be brought into consciousness where we can examine and change it. In this way we reprogram our operating system. This is the task of the crown chakra.

Other pieces of our core matrix are made up of things we have studied, learned, adopted, and then consciously chosen for our belief systems. These are spiritual beliefs, mastery of professional information, philosophical constructs, beliefs about oneself, likes and dislikes, skills, and our internal information bank of loosely associated pieces of pattern held in a subconscious filing system, waiting for deeper integration into the matrix. Each piece of information that our consciousness embraces gets filed through our matrix as we internally "search" for the appropriate place to attach the new information. If someone tells me they love me, I search my internal matrix for what that means. Each matrix is unique, however, and the meaning I ascribe to this statement may be different from that of the person saying it to me. Integration and assimilation are the process of absorbing new information into the matrix.

When something cannot be absorbed, consciousness scatters or fragments. Overwhelming experiences, such as war trauma, childhood abuse, or excessive stress overload the mental matrix and cause it to break down. In extreme situations, the natural cohesion of our thinking process may disintegrate into psychotic thought processes, multiple personalities, or a total rejection of the information through amnesia. In milder cases of stress, we experience difficulty focusing our attention, thinking clearly and calmly, or being rational when we want to be. New information may be rejected as "bogus" or ridiculous, simply because our matrix has no previously laid foundation for incorporating the information. Unless our matrix is strong and broad, it cannot assimilate new information, and the chakra shuts down.

The presence of order implies the existence of some kind of consciousness. When we take our attention away from a system for a long period of time, such as missing a week of work, or letting our housework lag, then it is likely that system will move towards entropy, into disorder. One of the strongest arguments for viewing planet Earth as a living, conscious being is the self-regulating and self-organizing properties of our biosphere. The absence of entropy over a period of billions of years suggests the existence of a massive consciousness, a theory known as the *Gaia Hypothesis*.

The very process of thinking is the act of leading our attention along lines of order. One thought leads to another, and another, and to the examination of the relationship between various pieces of the pattern we are perceiving. We are always following the pieces we can perceive, searching for an order to put them in (or running from the implications of the order they present!) Once we have internally woven a set of information fragments together into a workable order there is an enjoyable moment of understanding, the triumphant "Aha!" that implies a wholistic integration of a new pattern.

No act of creation or manifestation can proceed without the preconception of an order. It may be cellularly coded in DNA and therefore unconscious, or it may be the idea in a painter's mind, or the drawn blueprints for a new product. This conceptualization shapes the raw energy into its future form. If we attempt to manifest something, it is our consciousness that gives order and form to what we are creating. Our mind provides the seeds of manifestation just as the body provides the roots of consciousness, through our nervous system and perceptive organs.

Consciousness is therefore the ordering principle of the universe. In fact, we could say that order is both what consciousness *is* and what it *does*.

Consciousness

In the crown chakra, we often speak of "higher consciousness." This refers to perspective—one can see further from the mountain top than from within the forest. In terms of chakra levels, we have moved beyond perceiving "things" to the relationships they describe, to their patterns and their deeper metapatterns. Higher consciousness is not necessarily "better" but it is broader and this is in keeping with the pattern of expansion created by moving upward in the Chakra System. It is the embracing of larger and deeper metaphysical patterns of which our daily patterns are but subroutines. The view from the mountain top, however, cannot see the small flowers growing by the stream in the valley, and this view is equally valid and worth seeing.

This brings us once again to the issues of transcendence and immanence—both of which refer to consciousness in relation to the physical world. In transcendence we are moving away from the smaller patterns to embrace a deeper, broader point of view. We are moving upward toward the crown chakra leaving behind the limitations of the small, the physical, the individual. We can reach a meditative state of oneness through transcendent consciousness, a place of peace and understanding, leaving the body for the vast and unlimited realm of the mental planes. Transcendence allows us to escape, to rest, to renew ourselves with new perspective.

Immanence is the path of consciousness coming *into* the body. Immanence means that we pay attention to the here and now, to the specific and the finite. Through immanence we enliven and enrich, charging otherwise inert matter with divine intelligence. Through immanence, consciousness is creative, embodied, made manifest. Through immanence we challenge and change what we need to escape from and make the profane sacred. In balancing the Chakra System we seek to experience both.

Consciousness, however expansive, is an internal experience. A single human brain contains some 13 billion interconnected nerve cells capable of making more connections among themselves than the number of atoms in the universe. This staggering comparison presents us with a remarkable instrument. As there are 100 million sensory receptors in the body and 10 trillion synapses in the nervous system, we find that the mind is 100,000 times more sensitive to its internal environment than the external. It is truly from a place within that we acquire and process our knowledge.

Moving within is a way of accessing a dimension that has no locality in time and space. If we postulate that each chakra represents a dimension of smaller and faster vibration (higher frequency), we theoretically reach a place in the crown chakra where we have a wave of infinite speed and no wavelength, allowing it to be everywhere at once and yet having no perceivable location. Divine states of consciousness are described as omnipresent. By reducing the world to a pattern system occupying no physical dimension, we have infinite storage capacity for its symbols. In other words, we carry the whole world inside our heads.

To work on the crown chakra is to examine and expand our consciousness. We do this through expanding our information bank, by exploring and reaching out, by learning and study. We do it by examining our belief systems, our internal programming, and working the "bugs" out of our operating system. We do it through meditation, which allows our consciousness to turn within and transcend the smaller patterns of the mundane. And we do it through coming into our bodies, paying attention to the information that comes through our sensory receptors, and expressing our consciousness through the actions of the body. For these efforts we obtain clarity, sensitivity, intelligence, understanding, inspiration, and peace.

Excess & Deficiency

We all have known people who are "always in their head," who seem to know it all, who insist on being right, or who attempt to dominate others with their "holier-than-thou" attitude. These people have an excessive seventh chakra. They may be overcompensating in the seventh chakra to balance deficiencies in lower chakras. Their spiritual or intellectual elitism is often oppressive, although those with seventh chakra deficiencies may be drawn to them as followers. Excessive seventh chakras may "space out" frequently, or become overly detached or dissociated.

Those who have trouble thinking for themselves and rely on others to guide them are exhibiting seventh chakra deficiency. Narrow-mindedness and rigidity of belief systems keep us closed down and limit the expansion of consciousness characteristic of a strong seventh chakra. If we choose to maintain a state of ignorance rather than learning from our experience and seeking further insight and knowledge, we are acting from deficiency.

Spiritual abuse, or denying someone their own natural experience of spirituality by forcing on them a rigid system of beliefs, can create either excess or deficiency in this chakra. This abuse can close us to all spirituality, leaving us spiritually alienated or empty.

Just as the first chakra forms our roots in the material world, the seventh chakra is our connection to the spiritual world, the expansion of consciousness and the gateway to all that lies beyond.

Working with Movement

There are many movement systems designed to assist us in our journey towards enlightenment or spiritual consciousness. One of the best known is hatha yoga, in which many of the poses presented in this book have their origin. Others include T'ai Chi, Chi Kung, Sufi dancing, Arica, Peter Deunov's Paneurhythmy, and Chogyam Trungpa's Space Awareness, to name just a few. The fundamental premise is that our body is the most basic tool we have to work with towards higher consciousness. It provides a means of practice that uses all our physical and mental resources towards the goal of transcendence. This does not mean that we leave the body behind, but rather that our consciousness can expand beyond the narrow confines of the body, that we are not limited to the body.

Hatha Yoga

The chakra system has its origins in the system of yoga, and we highly recommend the practice of hatha yoga as a meditation technique focusing on the body. We specifically recommend the Iyengar approach to hatha yoga, as teachers trained in the tradition of B.K.S. Iyengar tend to have excellent training, not just in the formal poses, but in techniques for adapting them to all body types and levels of flexibility, strength, and balance. They are likely to be competent to help you work with any injuries or problem areas that might create problems if you are working just from a book or with a teacher who does not provide individual attention and correction. If you live in an area where Iyengar teachers are not available, the books mentioned in the Resources section of this chapter can get you started. These can act as an adjunct to any classes you might find, and could give you a means to practice alone if there are no teachers available at all, Iyengar or otherwise. If you do practice alone, you might consider joining a retreat or workshop for an intensive experience of modeling and correction by a teacher that you could then bring back to your solitary practice. Yoga Journal, a bimonthly magazine devoted to yoga practices, often lists workshops, seminars, conferences, and teachers in various areas of the world, and this may help you in your search.

Movement Meditation

This is an activity that has very few formal rules or structure. It allows you to spend time with your body, allowing it to dance in whatever ways it wants without consideration for style or appropriateness, but with attention to the body's signals to find the direction and quality of the movement. The dancer allows gravity and weight, momentum and breath, mood and energy level, to determine the dance. Here are some basic ideas for framing a movement meditation practice.

1. At least at first, practice alone. Allow yourself the luxury of completely letting go, leaving your self-consciousness outside the sacred space of your practice time.

2. Choose music that reflects your mood. Another alternative is to choose music that sweeps you away, compels you to move without consciously directing your body. Look for music that can pull the movement out from within you without distracting you from your own body's signals.

3. Focus on your breathing, expanding the capacity of your lungs, bringing in more fresh air and oxygen than ordinary shallow breathing allows.

4. Listen to your body signals, tuning in to information that is usually blocked out as intrusive (i.e. stiffness, pain, aches, itches) and find ways to ease the tension through movement and stretching. Experience freshly the skeleton, muscles, joints, and fluids that make up the physical body.

5. Find your center, your balance, and work with the body's weight and with gravity's effect on it, playing with momentum and the dynamics of motion.

6. Enter your practice without expectations. Allow your body to take you to where you need to be, rather than attempting to impose a preconceived idea of what your movements should look like or feel like.

7. Continue to practice a technique that offers your body training in alignment and appropriate movement (i.e. hatha yoga, Feldenkrais technique, Alexander technique), so that when you

surrender to your body's movement inspirations, it is capable of carrying them out without injury.

Other Approaches to Movement Meditation

Described below are two very different movement practices that are oriented toward meditation. Workshops and classes are available through the contacts listed.

Authentic Movement

This practice involves movement with a witness. There is a specific framework within which the interaction between the mover and the witness takes place, creating a safe space for the movement to manifest and be received by both. Although classes and teachers of authentic movement are found primarily within dance therapy circles, there is a deep awareness of this technique as a mystical and ritual practice. For information contact Michael Reid, 3217 14th Ave. S. #4, Minneapolis, MN 55407, (612) 729-4328.

Continuum Movement

Continuum is the movement and sound work of Emilie Conrad Da'Oud, who teaches workshops in her theories and techniques. She works with movement from a cellular level, starting with the very subtle energy movement that takes place within the body before working up to movements that might be seen by the naked eye. Workshop information is available through Susan Harper, 13432 A Beach Ave., Marina Del Rey, CA 90290, (213) 827-2704.

Putting It Into Practice

As we enter the crown chakra, we begin to examine the very process of consciousness itself. Where we have been feeling, acting, seeing or hearing, we now focus our attention on the act of thinking and the self-reflective awareness that can do such a strange thing as "think about its own thinking."

The experience of *Sahasrara* is the experience of the Divine, of our own Divinity within, and of union with the vast beyond. This is a process of opening to a higher, deeper or greater power—the essence of expanded consciousness, most often accessed through meditation techniques.

Meditation

There is no greater activity for opening the crown chakra than meditation. Listed below are several different kinds. If you don't already have a meditation technique, experiment with a few different ones until you find what works best for you. It is important when experimenting, however, that you use one technique regularly for a while before judging whether it is suitable for you. If you meditate every day, trying one for a week might be a reasonable trial period. If you meditate less regularly, you may wish to use one technique for a month or more before you can adequately experience its effects. Meditation, like many of the chakra exercises, is cumulative.

Tratakam (Gazing)

Sit comfortably in a dimly lit environment with your spine aligned on a chair, pillow or floor. Place a lighted candle centered in front of you, and simply focus your gaze and your attention on the candle flame, calming your breath and your mind.

Mantra Meditation

This is the technique popularized in this country by the Transcendental Meditation Society (TM). Sit comfortably, spine erect, in your favorite meditation posture. Calm your mind and focus your thoughts by picking a simple one or two syllable sound, and uttering it internally, very slowly, over and over again. Common mantras are sounds such as Om, So Ham, I am, etc. The idea is to internalize the mantra, and let its vibration create resonance (see Chakra Five) in your brain waves, breathing, and heartbeat.

Counting the breath

This meditation simply focuses the mind on the breathing. Sit comfortably and count your breaths, following them closely as they go in and out, in and out. Allow them to settle in a slow, steady rhythm.

Running Energy

This meditation allows the energy to run through you from above the crown chakra, down through each of the chakras, into the Earth. Think of the energy flowing down upon you and through you the way water flows out of a shower, lands on the top of your head and flows on down your whole body, and on down the drain. Like a shower, this is a cleansing meditation. The only difference is that we run energy through the *inside* of us, rather than just the outside.

Simply imagine your crown chakra opening like the lotus flower that its name implies. As it opens, imagine a shower of energy coming down from the Heavens into your crown chakra. You can visualize this energy as a shaft of light, a cool breeze, or the warmth of the sun, but make sure it is a kinesthetic experience of being infused with an energy source from above.

As it comes into your crown, it flows downward and runs through your third eye, your throat, chest, belly, genitals and perineum and right out of your body into the ground. When you get to the bottom, go back up to the top and get some more from this infinite supply within your imagination, and repeat the same downward flow of energy. Work towards feeling it flow through you in a constant stream, cleansing and soothing you.

Once you learn the basic meditation of running energy, then you can practice running different kinds of energy. You may choose to run hot or cool energy, male or female energy, red, blue or yellow energy. Each of these will produce a different kind of experience, and leave you in a slightly different state. You can pick an energy suitable to your needs at the time, such as running cool energy when you want to calm down from a tense day, or running powerful energy before a job interview.

Other Tasks

Do nothing for one day and spend it in complete silence and contemplation.

Fast for one day or several, removing yourself more from the material world. (This is not a task to be done lightly, and is not even suitable for some metabolisms. Be sure to check with your health practitioner to determine what is safe for you.)

Experience a sensory deprivation tank and observe your mind in the process.

Take a class in something intellectually or spiritually stimulating.

Go on a vision quest or spiritual retreat. This usually involves a period of time in the wilderness, often alone, in contemplative silence. How to do a vision quest is beyond our scope in this book. Check your local metaphysical bookstore for retreat centers or people who may be experienced at leading vision quests, or refer to the book listed in the reference section at the end of the chapter.

Study a new religion or metaphysical system.

Write an invocation or prayer.

Journal Exercises

1. Examining your Programming

Much of who we think we are—our values, our attitudes, our perceptions—develops through early programming by the models and teachers we have available at the time. This, of course, means that our parents or primary care-takers have an enormous influence on the thoughts we have about ourselves and the world around us and our ideas about how we should relate to it. Everything we come in contact with as we grow up influences the programming that we develop to process the overwhelming wealth of information coming in through our sensory organs at all times. Most of this processing occurs before the information reaches consciousness—we react to stimuli automatically, often not even knowing what we missed as our unconscious programs edited out the parts it decided we didn't need. (A wonderful book that expounds on this idea and provides ideas for stimulating consciousness and reprogramming is *Mind Magic*, by Bill Harvey, listed in the Resources section for this chakra.)

We begin the process of reprogramming by examining what programs are running things right now and where they came from. One approach to this is to list some of your beliefs on a piece of paper.

For each of the beliefs that you have listed, ask yourself the following questions:

• When did I first develop this belief?

• Who in my life, past or present, had a belief like this?

• Who would want me to have this belief?

• Do I have this belief to get their approval?

• What effect does having this belief have on my life and how I live it?

• How much happiness/unhappiness has having this belief brought me?

• Do I really believe this, or am I just following the programming I've been given?

• How do I feel about myself for having this belief? Does this belief fit with who I want to be now?

Journal Exercises

- What are the experiences I've had that have led me to developing this belief?

- What if I had not had those experiences, or had them knowing what I know now about the unconscious influence of that experience? What would I be like if I had not developed this belief?

- Do I want to continue believing this, or is there another belief that makes more sense to me?

2. Reassessment

- What have you learned about yourself as you've worked through the activities for the seventh chakra?

- What areas of this chakra do you need to work on? How will you do that?

- What areas of this chakra do you feel pleased with? How can you utilize these strengths?

Entering Sacred Space

Group Ritual
Materials Needed

Musical instruments

Circle of Divinity

Create sacred space in whatever way the group chooses. Place musical instruments (drums, rattles, sticks, bells, whatever anyone brings) in the center of the space or wherever participants will be able to get them later. Each participant finds a place in the room to work, not worrying about circle formation at this point. One participant leads the group in deep relaxation and the preparation for trance journey (pg. 245). A steady drumbeat is helpful for this, and if the person leading the visualization has trouble talking and keeping a steady beat, another person can be drummer. The guide then leads the group through the following :

Here in your inner temple, allow yourself to become still, emptying yourself of thoughts. Now that you have come to this empty, receptive state, you become aware of a presence, it may be outside of yourself, or it may be deep inside. You sense that this is divinity, this is something beyond your solitary existence as a single human being living this single life. You feel an openness at the top of your head, a softening of the boundary of your body, and then a sense of being entered, filled by something intangible, an energy that is vibrant and yet soft, flowing within and without you, connecting you to a universal source. At the same time, there is a resonance from deep within you, a sense of that same kind of energy swirling through you to merge with the limitless energy that has entered you. Feel yourself expand, every cell of your body alive and glowing, radiating. Allow your physical body to manifest this convocation of divine energy, moving as you breathe, allowing that radiant energy to guide your muscles and bones into a dance with the space around you. There is no one pattern for how this dance manifests, as it is different for each person, different each time we open ourselves to it.

(Take your time going through this, pausing between sentences, then leaving enough time for participants to work with the drumbeat on their own.)

Now let your movement bring you into a circle with the other dancers, choosing whatever rhythm instruments draw you and beginning to use them to join in the rhythm of the drum. One at a time, you will enter the center of the circle, dancing your dance as the rest of us match your movement with sound, playing wildly if you dance wildly, playing gently if your dance is a soft and quiet one. We each give the focus of our divine energy to the one in the center, supporting them with sound, celebrating the divinity that shines forth from them.

When all have had their turn, ground the energy and complete the circle in whatever way the group chooses.

Resources

Books & Magazines

Couch, Jean. *The Runner's Yoga Book: A Balanced Approach to Fitness*. Rodmell Press, 1990. (not just for runners—one of the best manuals around)

Foster, Stephen & Little Meredith. *The Book of the Vision Quest*. Sun Bear Books.

Hampden-Turner, C. *Maps of the Mind*. Macmillan.

Harvey, Bill. *Mind Magic: The Ecstasy of Freeing Creative Power*. Unlimited Publishing,1989. Available from Unlimited Publishing, Box 1173, Woodstock, New York 12498.

Kravette, Steve. *Complete Meditation*. Para Research.

McDonald, Kathleen. *How to Meditate: A Practical Guide*. Wisdom Publications.

Mehta, Silva, Mira & Shyam. *Yoga: The Iyengar Way*. Knopf.

Tart, Charles. *Waking Up: Overcoming the Obstacles to Human Potential*. Shambhala.

Tobias, Maxine & Stewart, Mary. *Stretch & Relax*. The Body Press.

Weinman, Ric. *One Heart Laughing: Awakening Within Our Human Trance*. The Crossing Press.

Yoga Journal , P.O. Box 3755, Escondido, CA 92033.

Conclusion

Understanding the Concept

Integration

Now that we have gone into each chakra in depth, we have a deeper level of understanding from which we can examine the system as a whole. It is here that we tackle the final and most important aspect of chakra work: integration.

None of the chakras function by themselves. As wheels spinning at the core of our being, the chakras are intermeshing gears, working together to run the delicate machinery of our lives. An imbalance in any particular chakra will affect other chakras, or may even be caused by them. Our power chakra is affected by the strength of our grounding. Our ability to open sexually may be influenced by our ability to communicate. Excessive attachment to power and control may interfere with love and relationships.

All of the chakras need to be open and functioning in balance with the others to be a fully thriving human being. We do not believe that any chakra is necessarily more important than another, or that we have to repress one chakra in order to open a different one. It may be important for an individual to focus on a particular chakra if that chakra has been underdeveloped in their life, but this is only for the purpose of overall balance in the system. It is also possible that a public speaker would want to emphasize her throat chakra, or an artist, his visual center. It is fine to emphasize our talents, as long as it is not to the exclusion of other areas of our lives.

Overall, we want our base chakras to be a strong and solid support for our spiritual growth. We want clarity, ease, and consistency to fall back on. We want support from our ground, enjoyment in our sexuality, and potency when we focus our power. We want a healthy body, full of feeling and vitality.

In the upper chakras we want freedom and flexibility, creativity, and expansion. We want new ideas, new information, and expansive time to reflect upon them. We want the inspiration that makes the survival routines of the lower chakras worth living. We want to be ever expanding our horizons, our knowledge, and our perceptions.

In the heart chakra, our core center, we want a sense of balance and peace—balance between our upper and lower chakras, balance between inner and outer, giving and receiving, mind and body. And we want that balance to allow an integration of these polarities, an integration that allows us to embrace a multiplicity of possibilities, and an abundance of love. From a point of balance in ourselves, we endeavor to enter into balance with others, both in intimacy and in our general social environment.

It is also important that all the chakras work together—that we communicate our visions, that we ground our power, that there is pleasure in our work and relationships, that there is continued learning on each level. As intermeshing gears, the chakras must be full enough to "touch" the ones above and below, and not so full that they are too overloaded to spin. If you look at the diagram on the following page, you can see how a deficient or excessive chakra can block the overall flow.

As we examine the system as a whole we can assess our overall energy patterns. If we are stronger in the upper chakras and weaker in the lower ones, then we are a top-down energy system. That is, we take in more energy at the upper levels and slowly transmute it downward. We might intellectualize something before we decide what to feel about it, or fantasize about things a long time before we act upon them.

A bottom-up energy system is just the opposite. Here is a person who wants to get all their ducks in a row before they expand to new territory. Security is important, as is physical manifestation. This person may spend a lot of time sorting out their feelings before they decide what to think. They may want to stick to the tried and true methods of their past and be resistant to trying new things.

Body types are often, though not always, indicative of the energy systems inside. Bottom-up persons will have a tendency to put weight on their lower body, or be heavy in general, while top-down types tend to be wiry and underweight, as they pull away from the physical. This is not always true, however, as many people with weight problems spend most of their time in their heads. In this case, the large physical body is an attempt at grounding and self-protection for a body that is only partially occupied. Coming to terms with the physical can help pull the

Top Down and Bottom Up Chakra Patterns

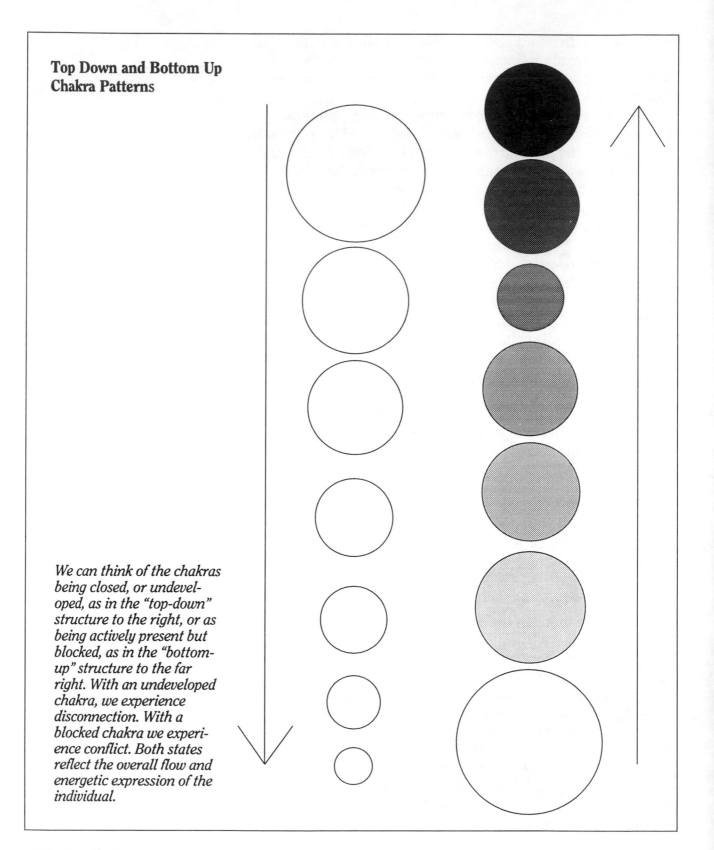

We can think of the chakras being closed, or undeveloped, as in the "top-down" structure to the right, or as being actively present but blocked, as in the "bottom-up" structure to the far right. With an undeveloped chakra, we experience disconnection. With a blocked chakra we experience conflict. Both states reflect the overall flow and energetic expression of the individual.

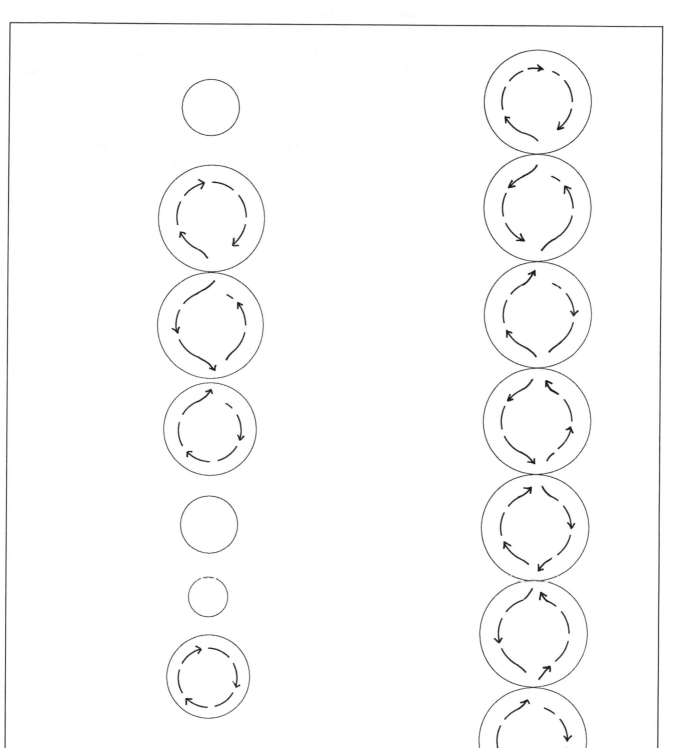

Chakras spinning as gears engage each other when large enough to touch. The serpentine path of energy running through the "gears" is symbolic of the oscillation of Kundalini energy.

body into better shape.

There is also a kind of mind/body split that exhibits a sense of being open on either end but closed in the middle. There may be good grounding, in the sense of a healthy body or ability to stick to a job, and a lot of imagination, creativity, or intellectual ability, with a blocked sense of being able to take action in one's life, or a fear of reaching out in relationships. This type of person tends to have contradictions in their life, a mixed sense of knowing their own self, or in the extreme, a kind of "split personality." The healing here is to connect mind and body and to address issues in the blocked chakras.

It is the human tendency to gravitate toward that which we do well and to avoid that which is difficult. The top-down person will be more likely to read books for personal growth than to take an aerobics class. Quiet types like to do yoga, while energetic types study martial arts. In working on chakra development, it is important to develop the areas in which we are weak. If meditation is difficult for you, keep trying to find a way to engage in it. If you abhor exercise, try to find something that makes it more appealing. After the initial resistance is worn away, you will most likely discover great value in your activity.

Where Are You Now?

Strengths & Weaknesses

When you've completed your journey through each of the chakras it is time to do an overall assessment of your whole system. In your journal, draw a line down the middle of the page, labeling one side *Strengths* and the other side *Weaknesses*. For each chakra write your assessment and examine how the strengths and weaknesses might affect one another. Be as honest as you can about where you are, even sharing your assessment with a trusted friend to see if your perceptions match with the perceptions of one who knows you well.

The Seven Rights

• On a scale of one to ten, how much do you feel you have re-claimed your seven basic rights associated with the chakras?

The Right to Have
The Right to Feel, The Right to Pleasure
The Right to Act
The Right to Love and Be Loved
The Right to Speak and Create
The Right to See
The Right to Know

• What work do you still need to do to claim these rights fully?

Looking at Relationships

Once we have a sense of our own overall balance, we can then examine how our chakra patterns manifest in relationships. Our inherent tendency is to seek balance consciously or unconsciously. If we cannot find it within ourselves, then we seek partners who will balance us in some way, most often unconsciously. Examining our chakra system in relation to another system can tell us where the most problems and benefits are likely to occur in the relationship.

While our unconscious tendency is to find balance with another person, and to gravitate toward that which we need to develop, it is also true that chakra patterns tend to perpetuate and reinforce themselves. Two people who have "top-down" structures may spend a lot of time intellectualizing, while "bottom-up" structures may reinforce attachment to the material world at the cost of other growth.

Draw a diagram of your own chakra system on the left and of your partner's chakra system on the right. Use a small, dark circle for a closed or deficient chakra, a large dark one for an excessive chakra. If the chakra is open and strong, then a large open circle would be drawn. Intermediate levels can be partially shaded. The size of the circle can reflect your assessment of the development of the chakra. You may also have a chakra that is basically open but conflicted, as in someone who is very sexual but has difficulty achieving orgasm, or someone who is very psychic but plagued by nightmares.

Now examine the two systems side by side. Open chakras next to each other will tend to reinforce each other, with a lot of energy being exchanged at these levels. A closed chakra will seek to draw energy from a partner's open chakra, such as an emotionally blocked person needing someone more open to help him sort out his feelings. Open chakras at opposite ends to your partner's will tend to balance, such as intellectual people gravitating toward their partner's groundedness.

Draw arrows between the chakras that are likely to have the most pull toward each other, and draw dotted lines between the ones that are most likely to have problems.

How does this drawing reflect your experience of the relationship?

What chakras are operating in the areas where you have the most problems in this relationship?

What chakra strengths could you draw upon to help combat these problems?

For additional information you might compare your partner's chakra structure to your parent of the same gender as your partner, and see if there are similarities or large differences. This exercise can also be done with your children, your boss, or a person you find particularly difficult.

Description of Chakra Relationship Diagram

In the diagram at right, person A is basically a "top-down" structure, with greater openness and development in the upper chakras. Person B is a "bottom-up" structure, with an out of balance fourth chakra. Stereotypically, we might imagine the middle American heterosexual relationship here, with A as the intellectual, assertive male, and B as the overgiving homemaker type, though such structures could occur with any gender.

A is attracted to the strong and solid ground of B, and what looks to be a very nurturing quality, due to the large heart chakra and moderately open second chakra. B is attracted to A's intellect, and there is a certain amount of matching in the areas of intuition and communication, as well as the basis for a good heart connection. The strongest tie will be between A's crown and B's solid base, as this will stimulate her intellectually and help him be in his body. This is a mutual connection.

Solid lines represent exchanges that are basically unidirectional, double lines are reciprocal energy, and dotted lines are conflicted exchanges. Because A is out of his body, his sexual energy is fairly blocked. B's second chakra is somewhat more open, with some blocks, and we might imagine that they would have sexual conflicts masked by her nurturing attitude towards him. A has a fairly strong third chakra, where hers is more blocked, so she may let him take the lead in most matters that require assertion. Not getting the pleasure she needs keeps her second chakra from stimulating her own sense of power. The blocked energy of the second and third spill out into the heart chakra which reaches out excessively in an attempt to bridge the gap by excessive giving in hopes that she might receive the love she needs. This excessive heart chakra smacks of codependence, which can make for conflicted heart connections mixed in with their otherwise strong heart connection.

Despite conflicts, there is a good deal to be said for this relationship. If A and B can turn their conflicts into opportunities for growth, they can each benefit from each other's strengths.

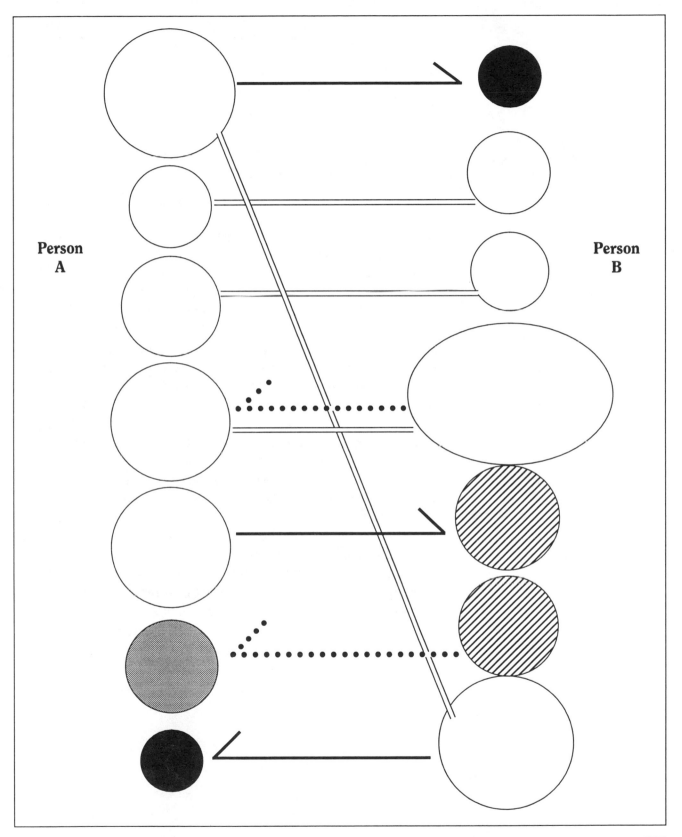

Person
A

Person
B

Working with Movement

Now that you have experienced the movement practices of each of the chakras, create your own chakra movement sequence by choosing one movement or pose from each. Work out graceful transitions between them and practice this sequence until you know it well. You can use this to take you through your chakra system whenever you like. You might include visualizations to go with the movement of each chakra, or use this sequence with the chakra six rainbow color meditation to intensify its effects.

Another approach might be to create a music tape for yourself with your favorite music for each chakra, a few minutes of each. You can then use this tape to inspire improvisation each time you want to experience the chakra journey through movement. The improvisational dance journey can be done without music as well, opening yourself to the movements that feel appropriate in each chakra at that moment, without the influence of music dictating what should be happening. This can be a diagnostic dance, providing you with information about what is going on in each chakra as you find it expressed in movement.

The most important thing to remember is that your body is an integral part of your understanding of yourself and your continuing growth process. Find ways to include movement in your ongoing practice and you will be rewarded by information about your state of being as well as connection with a source of pleasure and expression. A daily movement practice does not have to be strenuous in order to strengthen your sense of being fully in your body and fully engaged in your life and growth.

Putting It Into Practice

Daily Check-in

Do a mini chakra reading on yourself at the beginning or end of each day, or once a week. You could even chart your readings, if you are industrious, so that you can see whether there is a pattern. Just start at the bottom and ask yourself, "open or closed?" and mark it O for open and X for closed. You can also record how you are feeling at the time, how your life is going, what exercises you have or have not been doing, and any other correlations that seem pertinent.

If you see that one of your chakras is going through crisis, closing down, or otherwise needing attention, return to some of the exercises for that particular chakra and work on them for awhile. Remember, however, that all the chakras are interrelated and a problem is seldom the cause of one chakra alone. Be sure to ask yourself if another chakra could lend support (like working on grounding to decrease powerlessness).

Daily Practice

Daily meditations and cleansings are highly recommended. Simply find a quiet time to let your energy settle out. Breathing exercises (pranayama) are good for your energy and spirit in general, stimulating all the chakras. So is physical exercise, massage, lovemaking, fun, visual and audial feasts, and learning new things. The exercise in chakra six of visualizing each color of the rainbow in each chakra in turn is a good meditation for cleansing and energizing the chakras from a mental plane. Freeform dancing, yoga, or bodywork, are all good ways to energize chakras from a physical plane.

Daily Grounding

If you can only do one thing, we recommend daily grounding, especially with the Tree of Life meditation (see page 73). Pushing your energy downward into the earth and letting yourself get anchored can do wonders to bring everything else in alignment. Allowing the energy to then come back up and sprout out your crown chakra brings awareness to all your chakras.

Be sure to focus on the direction your energy needs to go in order to balance. This means that if you are basically a "top-heavy" energetic structure, more mental than physical, then it is best to focus on sending your energy downward through the chakras, into the manifesting current. If you are more grounded in your lower chakras, with a tendency to get sluggish or stuck, then you need to focus on the liberating current, moving your energy up from the bottom. In all things, balance is our goal.

Work with Others

Develop a class to share this material with others. There is no better way to learn something than to try to figure out how to teach it!

Integration

Be creative about how you integrate. There is no one right and only way. The best exercises are the ones that you develop for yourself because they work for you. (This is where we began with all this material!) If you basically understand the system, how you use it is only limited to your imagination. Have fun!

Entering Sacred Space

At the conclusion of our nine month intensive workshops, the students are asked to create their own ritual as a culmination of our work together. Each student chooses a chakra to work on, and each pair or group creates the segment of the ritual that will bring us through one chakra. We put them all together, bring food to share, and celebrate together.

If you have worked with a group to experience the chakra journeys we've presented, you could follow this example to create a ritual together. If you have worked alone, decide for yourself what you would like to do for each of the chakras and then perform your ritual for yourself. Alternatively, you might like to invite some interested friends and lead them through your chakra ritual.

Congratulations!

We end our exposition here, having entered sacred space to celebrate the completion of this round of the *Sevenfold Journey*.

Congratulations are truly in order! If you have worked your way, step-by-step, through this workbook, then you know better than anyone the work and dedication required. We sincerely trust that the growth and healing received have made the journey worthwhile.

Having completed this particular journey, we hope that you now have a solid framework for continuing further work in your life—that you will return to these exercises again and again—for chakras that give you particular trouble or for issues that may arise at different times in your life. The opportunity is yours to continue the Sevenfold Journey in your own way, revisiting familiar places in yourself as well as discovering new terrain with each turn of your inner wheels.

For truly, the journey of enlightenment never ends, but expands and transforms beyond a series of exercises and tasks to embrace your entire life. The framework of the chakras will permeate the activities of your days, your understanding of yourself, and your relationship to the world you live in. May your future excursions be full and joyous!

Resources

Workshops

Selene and Anodea teach a yearly *Chakra Intensive* workshop in California, and travel to other parts of the country for shorter weekend workshops. We also welcome feedback and suggestions on the material contained herein, as this is how our information has grown and developed over time. To write to the authors, or for further information about their workshops and classes contact:

LIFEWAYS, 2140 Shattuck Ave. Box #2093, Berkeley, CA 94704.

Tapes

There is also an accompanying meditation tape: *Journey Through the Chakras,* available through:

Association for Consciousness Exploration 1643 Lee Rd. Rm 9, Cleveland Heights, OH 44118.

Books

Anodea's first book, *Wheels of Life: A User's Guide to the Chakra System,* contains more extensive descriptions of the chakras themselves, delving deeper into the philosophy with less emphasis on the practice. It is available through:

Llewellyn Publications, P.O. Box 64383, St. Paul, MN 55164

Kasl, Charlotte. *Many Roads, One Journey.* Harper.

Levine, Stephen. *Guided Meditations, Explorations and Healings.* Anchor Books.

Macy, Joanna. *World as Lover, World as Self.* Parallax Press.

Small, Jacquelyn. *Transformers,* DeVorss.

Anodea Judith, a leading authority on the integration of chakras and therapeutic issues, is the author of *Wheels of Life: A User's Guide to the Chakra System*. She has an M.A. in Clinical Psychology and training in bioenergetics, acupressure and shamanism.

Selene Vega is an educator with an M.A. in Clinical Psychology. She presents classes and workshops in sacred dance and university seminars in movement therapy and addiction. Both authors live in Northern California.